Understanding and Reporting
Human Capital

In an era
of
integrated thinking

By
Nick A. Shepherd

ISBN 978-1-7775703-8-5

Written and published in Canada
using Kindle Direct Publishing by Amazon
Publisher Eduvision Inc. / Jannas Publications
Cover design by: KDP / Amazon
Edited by Frances Watkins

By the same author

Variance Analysis for Cost Performance Measurement (1980).
Governance, Accountability and Sustainable Development: An agenda for the 21st Century (2005).
The Controllers Handbook (2nd edition 2008).
Reflective Leaders & High Performance Organizations (jointly with Dr. Peter Smyth) (2012).
How Accountants Lost Their Balance (2021).
Corporate Culture – Combining Purpose and Values (2021).
The Cost of Poor Culture – The Massive Financial Opportunity in an Enhanced Workplace Culture (2021).

Dedication

To all the good, progressive human resources people that I have known but often disparaged over the years – this is for you. You were right and I was wrong!

This is also for the progressive people that I have had the pleasure to get to know, especially over the last ten years, who are driving a new agenda to develop human-centric thinking and develop organizations where the importance of people and the creation of a positive working environment are strategically focused.

Finally, to my wonderful wife, Janet, and my family. Thanks for your understanding and patience – even though many of you are still not sure what I actually spent my career doing.

Contents

Table of figures

There is no greater loss or waste in human society than the waste of human potential.

Human Capital Metrics

Executive Summary

This book focuses on the reporting of human capital, providing a framework for the understanding of people as an integral part of an organization's business model; it shows how the need for human capital reporting has evolved, where to start and where reporting needs to develop. It is presented in two parts: Part 1 addresses core concepts of human capital reporting and traditional HR-focused thinking, demonstrating what is changing and why this approach is no longer enough. Part 2 addresses the need for an evolved, strategically-driven, human-centric reporting approach that is broad-based, including culture and engagement. It also shows how a framework can be built and populated.

The terms "people," "human resources," and "human capital" are used in this book within the same context. Human capital is one of the six capitals established by the Integrated Reporting <IR> framework (the others being financial, manufactured, intellectual, social and relationship, and natural capital). These form the resource base of the "whole business model" used by <IR> for broad-based integrated reporting. This information will be helpful in building metrics that assist in populating the "people" aspects of an integrated report and meeting requirements such as those of the SEC[1] which, to date, has offered no prescriptive approach as to what should be included.

---

[1] SEC: US Securities and Exchange Commission

One of the challenges in reporting information about human resources is the recognition that people interact with, and have an impact on, all other areas of business activity. People build relationships with each other, suppliers, and customers; they own, use, and create intellectual capital; and they impact natural capital and social capital both by their personal behavior and by individual actions when acting under management direction. People also can create as well as utilize manufactured capital. Finally, people are one of the biggest consumers of financial capital.

Recognizing both this integrated nature and the importance of "people" reporting presents a challenge in defining boundaries. This book will attempt to focus on the impacts of people only to the degree that they have a strategic impact on business operations.

By the end of this book, the reader is expected to have a greater understanding of the breadth of human capital reporting; it presents a framework for approaching the development of meaningful metrics, together with several suggestions for applicable metrics, how they can be used and how they add value and knowledge to aid risk assessment and decision making.

PART 1

Part 1 covers the basic foundations for human capital reporting and demonstrates current approaches to developing metrics, including the evolution of guidelines issued by the International Standards Organization (ISO). In Part 1, we identify changes that are taking place and why significant developments in human capital reporting will be needed in the future – especially within an integrated reporting context.

1 Introduction

Writing about an emerging and rapidly developing new area of knowledge is a challenge; the potential audience may include people who are already well-versed in new ideas and developments, while others are just starting and yet others are not even interested at this stage.

Change can be likened to a comet, as illustrated in Figure 1.1: at the front is a small proportion of organizations who have either already adopted or are developing leading practices, although they may be experimenting and seeing what works.

| Late adopters / laggards | Early adopters / followers | Leaders and early adopters |

Figure 1-1 Evolution of change from leaders to followers

Behind them come the many others, who know that they need to do something and may be in either the investigation or early adoption phases. They might be following where organizations, advisors, or academics, for example, are suggesting they need to go. Finally, in the tail, are those – probably the largest number – who are "too busy" or not concerned; they may only start to take interest when adoption of the changes becomes mandatory, or when they realize its importance to their own organization for reasons that include brand and reputation, or social change.

This book attempts to provide something for all these audiences. There should be no judgment about where the reader believes they are on the continuum. As good consultants will say *"...change starts with the reality of where the client is today."* The reader may want to skim through and find out what is included here and start at a chapter that seems right for them; presenting and implementing the information can be thought of as a story and that is how it is presented. Early adopters may want to skim over the background as they already know much of it; they may also want to skip the early frameworks and ideas as they are already past that stage. It is personal – whatever works for the reader!

Human capital is unique for several reasons. People are not owned by an organization, and their services can be provided by different means – they may be full-time employees, contractors, working at suppliers, or even customers, part-timers, or retirees. People are also complex, generally independent, having their own values, thoughts, ideas, and approaches. Each person has a unique personality that makes people a challenge for managers and leaders.

Few people work for free, so there are significant financial implications in developing and managing a workforce; people are often the single largest consumer of cash in an organization. Because they represent a big cost, they often attract a great deal of attention, since spending so much money has a significant impact on an organization's financial performance. The result is that financially-driven decisions will affect people and have an impact on their performance.

People are also unique because their involvement in any organization makes then part of an integrated system. It is the performance of the whole system in carrying out the organization's purpose that defines its success or failure. The role of the most senior management executive – usually the CEO – is to act as the "Chief Integration Officer." This person can be likened to the master chef, or the conductor of the orchestra, who brings together all the resources available to them, including people, to optimize performance of the whole system.

A CEO must carefully balance the approach to using all the resources to generate consistent performance, while protecting the future integrity and capability of the system. (This means making it sustainable and resilient.) Effective CEOs already know that balance is the key to the longevity, sustainability, and success of their business model. A pure focus on financial outcomes, often driven by financial incentives, may result in depletion of human capital – perhaps not in traditional terms of numbers and talent, but certainly in motivation and productivity.

The world has been changing and there is a growing need to understand and account for people as a key component of an organization's resources. While the base business model remains the same (inputs, processes, outputs, and outcomes), the components of value creation have shifted. People are probably the most critical resource for several reasons. Sure, they consume a lot of cash, but they are also the drivers of organizational capacity and capability. They continue to provide the physical capability to operate equipment and create the products and services that generate revenue and earn profits; however, today their role has shifted to be the enablers of almost every aspect of total system capability.

People are at the heart of innovation and creativity, developing products and services that power future growth and market appeal. People need to collaborate and cooperate in a way that allows this to happen as rapidly as possible. The "system" needs to be structured to enable this. This process is helped by building relationships with customers (and potential customers) as well as suppliers, regulators, and others. People are also the major source of intellectual capital, which enables both creativity and capability building.

This evolution in thinking about people is leading to a desire for more accountability and reporting about the "people" aspects of an organization's activity. This is being reinforced by a societal desire for organizations to recognize, and take responsibility for, the impact that employment has on people's lives. This can range from concerns about health and safety, which increasingly include the effects of stress and behavior in the workplace, and the resulting impacts on the whole of society. There is an increased awareness of mental health issues and the societal challenges related to wealth creation and distribution, as well as the perceived values and behaviors of different organizations.

All this leads to a growth in human capital metrics. However, while most interested parties agree that more information is required, there are few specific metrics that provide any meaningful linkage between an organization's performance and its workforce. There is a proliferation of new metrics, whose value is questionable, but which are consuming increasing amounts of time to create and report.

Two key problems may be identified. First, the creation of metrics related to people management has traditionally been dealt with by HR (Human Resources). Typically, these metrics have focused on areas such as:

- statutory compliance (e.g. health and safety or employment equity);
- performance of the HR function (in terms of its internal processes of management); and
- high-level metrics of HR and people performance (e.g. headcount, turnover, absenteeism, HR costs as a % of total costs, training and development costs, employee satisfaction).

Most of these metrics are "numbers", which still seem to focus on HR management as opposed to the strategic role of people; there are few cases in which the numbers reported can be linked to the performance of the whole organization as an integrated system.

This brings us to the second challenge – to be effective, HR management needs to be changed to a strategically-driven, enterprise-level initiative. This change in approach can be compared to challenges in the past, when it was assumed that the quality management department was responsible for quality. Only when it was realized that *everyone* in the organization had an impact on quality – that it was a strategic, organization-wide commitment – did quality management become embedded as a way of doing business. This is where we are today in terms of people – it is a strategic, organization-wide commitment to people (often referred to as being "people-centric") that will elevate the management, leadership, responsibility, and accountability for people to the appropriate level.

Who are these people that the new metrics should address? Certainly, it is the shareholders who carry the investment risk, but there are also other stakeholders, such as employees, who must comprise the first group. Employees can be full-time, part-time, temporary, or employed on contract, but in all cases this group would be "under the control" of direction from Management. But, since "stakeholder" typically refers to anyone who is impacted by or has an impact on the affairs of the organization, this spreads the net much wider, to include:

- employees (impacted by the direct "control" and leadership from the organization);
- families of employees (impacted by the effect that the organization has on the employee);
- people who work in any part of the supply chain (impacted and affected by decisions and behavior of the organization);
- people who work for clients and all "outbound" aspects of connecting the organization to the marketplace (impacted by the decisions and behavior of the organization); and

- people in wider society (impacted by the decisions and behavior of the organization).

The reason for the broad inclusion is that every one of these people is part of the business model through which an organization operates. Successfully engaging with all these people, especially in a service / knowledge economy, will have a positive impact on productivity, performance, sustainability, and value creation. Not engaging can have a negative impact.

Metrics can be a thorny issue and can create some level of resistance. Maybe some experiences will describe the challenge.

During my consulting career we had a long-term relationship with a privately owned, multi-national organization. Our initial work was team development with the senior leadership team and this evolved into strategic planning, including the development of key performance indicators (KPIs). We started with the senior executive team, but the work soon expanded to include general managers. At one team session (held at a hotel in Los Angeles, if I remember correctly), we were discussing the development and implementation of some new performance indicators and there was push-back from a number of participants; one in particular, a plant manager from Wales, at one point stated, *"you don't fatten the pig by continually weighing it."*

His comment brought laughter but did also provide some pragmatic clarity and focus to the discussion. Having thought about this since then, I have come to realize that we do, in fact need to "weigh the pig" but this is in fact a "total system" outcome measure. However, there is no causal relationship between the weight, and how it may change with respect to any particular action that is taken. This is a key dilemma of developing metrics, and KPIs in general, and one which we will discuss later. It is the foundation of the "input, activity, output, and outcome" framework that will be used.

I also remember another consulting assignment that we undertook in South Africa with a public sector organization. It was a progressive group, comprised of extremely bright individuals, who were implementing and using some key "knowledge economy" tools in their management toolkit; as an example, they had developed a core knowledge management system for both collecting and disseminating information internally, which was linked to their compensation and time-management systems.

Another tool they used was a framework that linked high-level outcomes and their metrics to core processes, projects, activities, and tasks through which these would be achieved. Through this approach, there was a clear "line of sight" between their intentions and expectations (goals and objectives), and the allocation and management of resources (strategies and tactics) required to achieve these. Their system was based on the concepts of RBM (Results Based Management). Every metric had some level of causal or relationship linkage from the highest-level outcome (goal) to the lowest-level task and activity.

If we think about "weighing the pig" and results-based management, we can establish the foundations for an effective approach to developing metrics. Firstly, let's look at the pig's weight: this is an important output indicator. If the pig is getting heavier, it suggests that things are going well; however, if the weight is not increasing at the rate required, then more information is needed about the causal factors that may be contributing to this. Only then can management take action to make the required changes. The outcome in this case might be "achieving top quartile results for pig at auction."

In the early days of quality management, organizations were quite good at measuring outputs and inputs. Final inspections ensured that there was compliance with requirements, and inputs focused on ensuring that all incoming materials were 100% inspected. Process control was about supervising workers, ensuring equipment was available and operating, and that defects and failures were being tracked (Figure 1.2). How does this compare to the current level of maturity in HR management and metrics? While it may be contentious, it appears that we are still only at the early stages.

Factor	Immature	Mature
Process centric management (task oriented) (1980 / 90 shift)	• Poorly planned process • Little documentation • Sporadic / unplanned training • Focus on final inspection • Compliance to final specification • Measure volume, defects • Fix after failure • Hidden costs of failure • Functional approach	• Detailed planned process • Documented and controlled • Structured training • Tools such as 6 Sigma / SPC • Focus on process control • Compliance at every stage • Stop and fix • Failure costs tracked • Enterprise approach (TQM)
People centric management (behavior oriented) (2020 / 30 shift)	• People as a cost / commodity • Control at macro cost level • Directed purpose • Goal driven • Directive, controlling • Scheduling, planning • Subservient to task • Based on management • Functional approach (HR) • Hidden costs of failure • Hidden risks to sustainability	• People as investment • "Valued" investment • Shared purpose • Values / culture driven • Participative, engaged • Talent management • Equal to task • Based on leadership • Enterprise approach • Failure cost known • Known risks to sustainability

Figure 1-2 Evolution of change – improved process to people engagement

It was necessary for process management to mature for organizations to remain competitive in the 1980s and 1990s. While outputs typically met specifications, outcomes fell short. Poor quality was causing excessive underlying costs, and activities like rework and repair were leading to late deliveries and, thus, dissatisfied customers. Outputs were satisfactory but outcomes were poor – including the declining market share.

Understanding the contrast between human capital and people management is the issue. This comparison further develops the idea of total quality management (TQM) into total people management (TPM). As we will see, although we have started with the basic understanding of the HR perspective, mature "human centric" organizations account for the fact that people issues are pervasive, affecting every aspect of organizational activity.

There seems to be a split in the evolution of human capital metrics between internal metrics, focused on effective management of human resources internally, related to resource allocation and decision making, and external metrics that inform investors (and everyone else) how important people are to the organization's operations and strategy, and how well they are being managed as a key resource. In Chapter 3, "The basic foundations," we will discuss the International Standards Organization guideline ISO 30414:2018 *Human resource management — Guidelines for human capital reporting for internal and external stakeholders*, but will focus on the foundation for *external* reporting.

However, before we embark on the big picture of both internal and external reporting, we need to step back and take a new look at what we are trying to achieve through any type of human capital reporting. This will be a holistic approach and will therefore create the basis for possible future development of *both* internal and external metrics.

Therefore, the first section of this book provides the background on the shift that is taking place and why this is changing the need for under-standing the impact of people on organizational performance. We explore progress to date and the important role that traditional HR reporting must play as part of the solution. Later chapters will outline the unique aspects behind creating an effective environment for people to operate and contribute at their highest potential. This is necessary because there are two parallel aspects to people management – talent *and* work environment (culture) – that are critical to ensure effective reporting of key performance.

This concept sets the course for understanding a much wider "enterprise view" of metrics. This includes a framework for metrics which reflects the types of information that should help stakeholders understand the strategic importance, quality, health, and risk related to people. In the final chapters, the book presents some thoughts on the challenges in measuring enterprise performance together with some comments on the issue of culture and human behavior.

A final word – and an admission: My personal focus and interest are on the emerging frameworks and approaches to human capital reporting that are described in the latter part of this book. The good news is that the importance of human capital has been recognized and is increasingly a requirement of corporate accountability. However, the bad news is that, while we may think we are well-established on the "journey," and many are already calling for standardization in ESG reporting, which seems to suggest that we know what is needed and what we are doing, this is not the case. While we have made some progress, we have not yet made any headway in true, integrated reporting that reflects inputs, activities / processes, outputs, and outcomes in anything other than financial terms.

I believe that significantly new approaches will be needed. We need to step back from the current approaches and re-think what must be done. In this respect, two major shifts are needed: First the temptation to churn out traditional HR metrics should be avoided, other than as a "stepping stone" toward the desired end; and second, the concept of "value" in financial terms must be balanced against outcomes that cannot be expressed in financial terms but are, nevertheless, critical for a sustainable organization. We must, once again, expand our thinking.

2 The evolving need for HR reporting

People have always been important to business. In the agricultural age, human labor performed much of the physical work, while the landowner was more likely to be educated and literate and, as such, typically provided the financial capital (and the "assets" – the land, materials etc.), made all the decisions and provided the direction and control. However, even at this stage, good landowners recognized the value of an experienced farm hand who had grown up on the land and understood the soil, crops, animals, weather and seasons, and many other practical realities that can only be gained from hands-on experience.

As machines were developed, people remained important, but fewer were employed as the machine took over manual tasks. With the coming of the industrial age, machines formed the foundation and investors provided the increasingly large amount of capital to establish factories and install equipment. The technology was mechanical, so human labor continued to be important, but education levels required were not high and many jobs were considered unskilled labor. There was no welfare state nor any kind of unemployment or medical insurance, so jobs were critical for most people to survive. Employers had the leverage, and job satisfaction in most cases really meant "be happy you have a job." Trade unions developed to provide some level of off-set to employer's leverage, and this helped to change working conditions which sometimes led to improvements for the workforce. Many such improvements were eventually built into employment legislation, particularly those related to areas such as health and safety, the working week, holidays, overtime, and other benefits.

However, these basic standards for working conditions were (and are) by no means global.

The next major change was the evolution of the service economy. While the industrial economy continued to grow, it was supplemented by the expansion of services, firstly in the "trades," such as mechanical engineering, plumbing, electrical services, gas and energy development and delivery, and the construction and building trades. These were then supplemented by other services, such as retail, banking, insurance, medical care, warehousing and transportation, and food services. As developed economies created more wealth, the marketplace and demand for services grew significantly.

This shift began to create an increased demand for skilled and semi-skilled people (which in turn led to growth in the education sector). A key aspect of this shift was that the individual now had increasing leverage because they had skills that employers needed. This was not new – many of the original trades had already realized this value and many of the old guilds for trades such as stonemasons or carpenters controlled both the numbers of new people able to qualify and the provision of labor to the employer. In this way, they controlled competition which ensured demand and reasonable pay levels. This is where the trades unions originated. Employers now had less leverage but there remained large numbers of people who lacked personal skills or qualifications, and who were "quickly and easily interchangeable" by an employer. There continued to be many jobs for which unskilled and semi-skilled employees made up the majority of the workforce.

Two major changes occurred in the 20th century. First, in the 1970s, the rapid development of technology led to increasing levels of automation. This rapidly impacted the complexity of manufacturing machinery and equipment, leading to a decline in demand for unskilled people. This was offset by a massive increase in demand for skilled and semi-skilled people, who could utilize the technology / operate the machinery to enhance organizational performance. While such people were needed by organizations to enable their growth and development, it was soon realized that talent was not enough. Alternative working environments were needed in which skilled people would be motivated to contribute and produce. Furthermore, managing and leading a "knowledge age" organization would turn out to be hugely different.

In their book *"How Google Works,"*[2] Eric Schmidt and Jonathan Rosenberg state, *"While we were brought into Google to provide 'adult supervision,' to succeed we ended up having to relearn everything we thought we knew about management and our best teachers were the people who surrounded us every day at Googleplex."* They go on to say, *"We both came to Google as seasoned business executives who were pretty confident in our intellects and abilities. But over the humbling course of a decade, we came to see the wisdom of John Wooden's observation that 'it's what you learn after you know that counts.'"*

The second major change was global competition: between 1950 and 2020, world trade grew by a factor of 274. This was enabled by expanding applications of technology to communications and logistics but was also driven in more recent decades by the competitive need for cost reduction that led to outsourcing of labor. Growth was also enabled by the removal of trade barriers and the emergence of economies that could offer low labor costs. As this strategy increased, it soon became apparent that many organizations and countries within which these facilities operated had poor labor standards. Reports of safety issues, fires, equipment failures, child employment, strong autocratic leadership, together with laws and practices that forbid employees to organize, all contributed to scandals.

To address the issues, there was a growth in Corporate Social Responsibility (CSR) and the introduction of a certification standard (SA

---

[2] Schmidt, Eric and Rosenberg, Jonathan, *How Google Works*, 2014, Grand Central Publishing.

8000) that progressive suppliers could obtain certification against. Again, this development of "good HR practices" continued and included the international standard, ISO 26000 *Guidance on Social Responsibility*. These macro-level changes started to draw attention towards the importance of people, leading to corporate governance, accountability, and reporting.

Historically, financial reporting has dominated corporate governance and accountability. This was because financial capital, money, was the key resource requirement for both setting up and sustaining a "going concern."

While the last 30 or more years has seen the continued importance of financial capital, "people" have emerged as a key strategic resource that drives an organization's capability to operate. Among the many reasons for this are: the growth of the service economy; the development of technology, especially computer and communications capabilities; and the growing importance of ideas and innovation as drivers of growth and prosperity.

While financial capital has remained critical, _where it is being spent has changed considerably_. Around 40 or more years ago, the financial balance sheet reflected a reality in which tangible assets – plant and equipment – formed the core area of investment required to create a business model; at that time, some 83% of an organization's value was "on the balance sheet." This is where the investors money was being directed - and it was clearly visible.

This represented a large portion of the financial value of the organization. Since then reality has changed. An increasing amount of cash has been invested in intangibles, as can be seen in Figure 2.1. Now the financial reports reflect very little of an organizations value - in terms of what money an investor has "at risk."

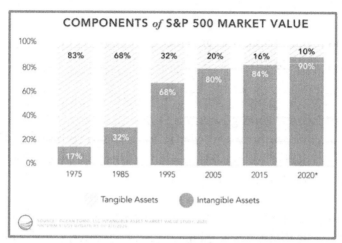

Figure 2-1 Growth of intangibles including human capital. Source: Ocean Tomo LLC

A large portion of these intangibles do not show up as assets in the financial records, resulting in today's balance sheet only showing about 10% of the value of the average organization. Much of the remaining 90% is the value created by human capital and retained in the form of hidden assets, such as relationships, value of the workforce, and organizational knowledge.

Much of this is not particularly new – ideas were always important and drove every economic revolution in the past; what IS new, is the scale and speed of the need for organizations to adapt to competitive pressures because of globalization and the speed of change. Not only are organizations looking for leadership in innovation and creativity, but they also seek customer involvement and satisfaction, high quality, low prices and therefore lower costs, and the agility to change and adapt at high speed. Almost all these strategic imperatives require people who are qualified, engaged, and committed both to the work they do and to the direction and goals of the organization.

This desire for information about the human aspect of organizational activity started with the company Ben and Jerry's Ice Cream, which produced their first "Triple Bottom Line" annual report in 1987, addressing people, planet, and profits.

There was also a growing realization that employee behavior was important; corporate (and governance) practices around the world vary, and issues of fraud, bribery and corruption started to be recognized on a broader scale. This led to legislation such as the Foreign Corrupt Practices Act enacted in the USA in 1977.

The issue of employee behavior has remained an ongoing theme since that time, with organizations developing codes of conduct, codes of ethics and ethical practices, and other guidance to frame expected behaviors. Ethical issues continued, sometimes at the highest levels, again bringing the realization that employee engagement and commitment was critical, while effective leadership was also crucial to ensure the desired behavior happened. Continued scandals led to reporting changes, such as SOX (Sarbanes Oxley) in the United States but, in reality, employee behavior remains a challenge. One strategy to address this is the growing focus on "corporate culture."

Many of these organizational changes were evolving in parallel to environmental concerns around, for example, acid rain, global warming, and climate change. To reflect this, many organizations started to develop and issue supplemental annual reports, in which, initially, environmental reporting was the main driver. In 1992, the UN Framework Convention on Climate Change (UNFCCC) was released and eventually signed by 197 countries. This led to various legislative demands for environmental reporting, as well as the development of "leading practises" that started to be reported. The shift in focus on reporting content can be seen from the chart (Figure 2.2).

Emerging Trends: Type of report	1992	2008
Social / community reports	8%	4%
Philanthropy		2%
Integrated (Financial + Non-financial)		5%
Sustainability (Environmental+Social+Economic)		33%
Corporate Responsibility (EHS+Community +Social)		32%
Environment, Health & Safety and Community		2%
Environment, Health and Safety	12%	3%
Environment and Social		3%
Environment	80%	14%

Figure 2-2 The changing focus of supplemental reporting 1992–2008

During this period, various voluntary frameworks had been developing for "non-financial" reporting. The challenge was that several countries had *different statutory requirements* and other groups, such as investors, were also beginning to ask for additional information. Shareholders were concerned about environmental issues and started requiring information as part of the Carbon Disclosure Program (CDP). In the USA, regulators were looking for guidance, and the Sustainability Accounting Standards Board (SASB) was created and started to issue guidelines. Various countries and regulators started to become increasingly concerned about the variety of information and the lack of consistency; this was one of the key reporting areas that framework developers, such as the Global Reporting Initiative (GRI) moved into, creating a great foundation of recommended approaches.

The reporting challenge had also become more complex because organizations were faced with different statutory demands for reporting financial information, environmental issues, and health and safety. There was also an evolving framework of leading practices, such as the GRI. Overlying all of this was the social feedback that organizations were tracking, through which society was looking at other areas related to corporate accountability. The four main topics and the maturity of guidance are shown in Figure 2.3.

Reporting area	Statutory	Leading Practices	Optional
Financial	Global and / or national standards	Limited	Limited
Environmental	Some - national	Yes - e.g., GRI	Yes
Health & Safety	Some - national	Yes	Yes
Social (Community / philanthropy, ethical)	Limited	Yes - e.g., GRI	Yes

Figure 2-3 Reporting topics and maturity of guidance

While financial reporting had some 100 years of maturity behind it, and was also well supported by both legislated requirements and globally or nationally accepted standards, most other reporting was a patchwork of nationally developed approaches, in addition to developing frameworks for leading practices, supplemented by what each organization felt was important to its own investors and owners, and its reputation and credibility.

By 2012, it was becoming apparent that the traditional financial reports and the various emerging supplemental reports that now addressed several issues, including aspects of "people," needed to be brought together. An international committee was formed, the International Integrated Reporting Committee (IIRC), to research, consult, develop, and propose a new framework for corporate reporting. The IIRC issued its first framework in 2013, and this was followed by several years of experimentation until the issue of updated guidance in early 2021. The recommended approaches have been gradually making their way into mainstream corporate reporting.

Global concern about the impact of organizations, especially global businesses, on society had also been growing. In 2015, the UN issued its

Sustainable Development Goals (SDGs), also known as the Global Goals, which were adopted by all United Nations Member States. This was a universal call to action to end poverty, protect the planet, and ensure that all people enjoy peace and prosperity by 2030.

While the SDGs did not have mandatory reporting status, they did begin to influence social policy on a national basis. Given the importance of the corporate sector in many of the UN goals, these also began to influence corporate reporting, as well as national policy and legislation.

Since Ben & Jerry's issued their ground-breaking report on People, Planet and Profit (the triple bottom line), there has been a continual process of voluntary adoption of broader reporting approaches to supplement financial information. There has also been significant development, during the same period, of reporting frameworks for voluntary adoption, as various stakeholders started to ask different questions related to risk, reputation and sustainability.

Figure 2.4 illustrates some of the key milestones in non-financial accountability and reporting that, to some level, have had an impact on human capital. As shown, the changes have evolved over the same period as the shift to focusing on intangibles as a basis of organizational value. The list illustrates the evolutionary process in the reporting of human capital. It was not until the GRI developed its guidelines in 2000 (that have since been defined as standards), that any level of prescriptive require-ment as to what was to be reported had been developed. Even the IIRC <IR> framework, which is probably the latest (revised 2021), and is becoming the de facto reporting standard, has not attempted to provide prescriptive requirements.

Organization / Framework	Start	Comments
	1971	Concept of "social contract" developed
SA 8000	1989	Standard issued by Social Accountability International, responding to working conditions at non-traditional
TBL	1994	"Triple Bottom Line" John Elkington
GRI	1997	Founded by CERES, UN and Tellus Institute
Corporate Register	1998	Corporate Register launched as global repository of CSR reports (for sharing / learning). Starts CRRA Awards in 2007.
SIGMA project	1999	Launch of The SIGMA project, DTI (UK), AccountAbility (and others)
GRI	2000	GRI - first set of guidelines followed by 2002 release of reporting details
ACCA / CERES	2002	Launch awards for sustainability reporting in US
AA1000	2003	Series of standards issued by SustainAbility
SIGMA project	2003	Launch of reporting model that incorporated "People" and other non-financial aspects.
ISO	2010	Issues ISO 26000 the first international standard on corporate social responsibility.
IIRC	2010	International Integrated Reporting Council, Accounting for Sustainability Project, GRI, and the International Federation of Accountants.
SASB	2011	Launch of Sustainability Accounting Standards Board
IIRC / <IR>	2013	Issue of <IR> framework for 6 capitals based reporting (updated 2021)
ISO	2018	Release of ISO 30414 Guidelines for internal and external human capital reporting (supported by several technical specifications since that date)

Figure 2-4 Evolution of supplemental reporting and guidance

However, by 2021, the world has reached a stage at which human capital reporting is moving beyond voluntary disclosure and is starting to be embedded in statutory reporting. The SEC has clearly signaled its intended requirements for disclosure, and SASB is moving ahead with investigating added guidance. Various business organizations have issued their own guidance, and the European Union is updating its requirements too. This will result in not only the continued development of metrics but also a "jockeying for position" as to what specific metrics will be required.

As this process evolves, it is sometimes hard to step back and ask: What are we trying to do here? The process of developing ISO standards, technical specifications, and guidance documents, for example, takes time. Focusing on implementing these standards is a great "early stage" approach, but there is a risk that it may still fail to account for the "big picture".

Evolving need – summary
• Expanded corporate accountability and reporting has been evolving for almost 50 years.
• People, Planet and Profit was one of the early approaches to including "human capital" (the Triple Bottom Line).
• Most supplemental reporting has been discretionary, so little standardization exists.
• The behavior of organizations, especially global businesses, has been of increasing interest as a societal issue.
• Social concerns related to people, working conditions, and human impact have been developing.
• Various recommended supplemental reporting frameworks have been evolving.
• The demand for broader "people" accountability is starting to show up in mandatory compliance requirements.
• Recommended standards and guidelines for reporting human capital are starting to emerge.
Evolving need – checklist
• Is the organization aware of the need for and importance of enhanced human metrics?
• Is the organization aware of the growing "big picture" evolution of corporate accountability?
• Is the organization aware of the emerging guidance of reporting on human resources / human capital?
• Has the organization started to review its approach to human capital as its dependence on people has grown?

3 The basic foundations

The business world is at the stage where human capital reporting is going to be required and, at some point, these requirements are going to become prescriptive. As in all new initiatives or requirements, there is a need to start somewhere. This chapter will focus on the need for external reporting. Almost every country, and even some states within countries, will have different compliance requirements related to human capital – such as health, safety, equality, and minority employment – already in place. Metrics demonstrating compliance in these areas will typically already be available. In this chapter, we therefore look at examples of where to start, where things seem to be headed, and what reporting structures already exist. The following are some starting points and existing guidance documents:

- Use what is already in place (do not "re-invent the wheel"!).
- Public company reporting requirements – possible directions:
  - US WIDA 2021 draft legislation / SEC guidance
  - Indian National Securities guidelines 2020
  - Existing and potential future European directions
- The existing (and proven) GRI reporting framework.
- ISO 30414 *Guidelines for Internal and External Human Capital Reporting*.

For many organizations, there will already be internal metrics that have been developed and are used to monitor the performance of traditional approaches to human resources. Some may have made it to the governance area of reporting at board level – and these may already be publicly disclosed. Thus, there needs to be a "thinking process" around the steps to getting started; more importantly, this should help avoid duplication of effort, i.e. "re-inventing the wheel," which often creates more work than needed.

#	Source	Detail
1	Statutory	Existing compliance to issues related to "people" management - safety, employment etc.
2	Internal HR Reports	Existing people management numbers wherever already used in the organization.
3	Existing non HR reports	Certain existing internal compliance activities require reporting e.g., ISO 9001 requires information on competencies, skills, and training records.
4	Government reporting	Many organizations already collect and report data to governments such as quarterly and annual reports on payroll and employment.

Figure 3-1 Potential sources of existing human capital metrics

Looking at the four areas of potential sources (Figure 3.1) will provide a portfolio of existing metrics that are available for incorporation into future reporting. One important approach that many organizations may already have in place, is likely to have come as the result of the work of Kaplan and Norton in *"The Balanced Scorecard."*[3] This concept identified the need to measure more than financial performance. While this book, focusing on the need to expand reporting metrics, was mainly intended for internal reference, it became equally applicable to external reporting.

---

[3] Kaplan, Robert. S., and Norton, David. P., *"The Balanced Scorecard,"* 1996, Harvard Business Press.

To place Kaplan and Norton's book in context, it was written at a time – the 1990s – when intellectual capital and knowledge management were becoming recognized as the drivers of value creation (and before the financial crash in 2000 when people started to recognize that financial disclosure did little to provide insights into valuation risk management). Writers such as Leif Edvinsson, Michael Malone, Thomas Stewart, Karl Sveiby and Anne Brooking were all seeking ways to understand and measure its contribution to organizational performance, publishing books that focused on what we now know as human capital.

Other books (refer to the Bibliography) laid many of the foundations for the approaches that are still being used today. Jac Fitz-enz is considered a pioneer in this field; others, such as David Weiss, and Messrs. Brain Becker, Mark Huselid and Dave Ulrich, also added to the thought processes of measuring human capital. Given that this was all over 20 years ago, many organizations will now have either dashboards or scorecards that include human capital metrics.

As a reminder, Figure 3.2 shows the four major aspects of scorecard reporting identified by Kaplan and Norton that, together, should provide a broader picture of organizational performance. Human capital was represented by the bottom right quadrant that focused on "learning and growth" as one of the four strategic drivers.

The Balanced Scorecard Institute (BSI), explains, *"This perspective includes employee training and corporate cultural attitudes related to both individual and corporate self-improvement."* In a knowledge-worker organization, people — a major repository of knowledge — are the main resource. In the current climate of rapid technological change, it is becoming necessary for knowledge workers to be in a continuous learning mode. KPMG in its next 20 years predictions included "Lifetime learning will become a human need." The need for understanding and measuring learning and its' related investment will grow exponentially[4].

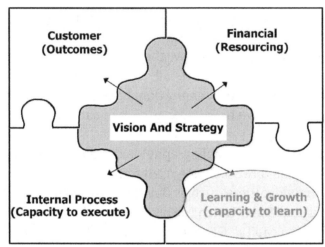

Figure 3-2 Four components of a scorecard

Metrics can be put into place to guide managers focus training funds where they can help the most. In any case, learning and growth constitute the essential foundation for the success of any knowledge-worker organization. We will return to the evolution of thinking around the scorecard later; at this stage, the concept might form the basis of existing approaches to human capital reporting within an organization that can quickly be adopted. That is, it sows the seed of the strategic importance of employee learning and development as a key metric.

Once we have an inventory of what metrics are already available, the next step might be to evaluate the sort of direction that future mandatory reporting is calling for. While most of such reporting currently pertains to publicly listed organizations, it provides a foundation for setting priorities. Here again, different countries may have issued different guidelines. Existing SEC requirements include basic information on number of

---

4 https://home.kpmg/ca/en/home/market-insights/predictions.html (extracted Nov 2021)

employees by broad category, but then recommends that anything material to investors also be disclosed and / or discussed. The following is a summary of the draft legislation in the USA to be recommended to the SEC based on the Workforce Investment Disclosure Act of 2020:

- Workforce demographics – full-time, part-time, contingent.
- Workforce stability – turnover voluntary / involuntary, internal hiring and promotion by diversity.
- Workforce composition demographics by ethnicity, race, gender.
- Skills and capabilities – average hours of training, training $ by employee, skills gaps, skill / strategy alignment.
- Culture and empowerment – harassment incidents.
- Health and safety – frequency, severity, time lost due to injury, illness, or fatality; fines under OSHA; actions under S 13. OSHA to prevent danger; actions under S. 11 (c) of OSHA.
- Compensation and incentives – total compensation and disaggregated data by demographic (FT, PT and contingent).
- Recruiting and needs – new jobs created, classification of new jobs, quality of hire and new hire retention rate.

Some of these suggested metrics are national in nature, related to legislation applicable to the USA; however, many are generic. These metrics are also supported by other human capital disclosure requirements in narrative form related to relevant policies and procedures.

The generic metrics appear to focus on "social accountability" more than anything else. One might argue that certain metrics are indicators of the health of an organization's "value creation" model, such as skills and capabilities. Also, some are related to "health of the work climate," such as culture and empowerment, and workforce stability. However, for the investor, there is no clear linkage between the HR metrics suggested and the sustainability of the organization's ability to create value.

How does this compare to other national approaches? The Securities and Exchange Board of India (SEBI) recently released guidance to the top listed companies requiring disclosure, which included areas such as:

- Details of employees – by permanent / other and gender.
- Differently-abled employee data – full-time and part-time.
- Representation of women – directors and senior management.
- Turnover rate – male and female.
- Complaints and grievances filed – status of complaints; shown by communities, shareholders, other investors, employees and workers, customers, value chain partners and other (to be specified). Includes working conditions or health and safety.
- Training and awareness around conduct of business including ethics – numbers and % of category trained in board, key management positions, other employees, and workers.
- Penalties and fines paid for non-compliance to regulators, law enforcement agencies and judicial institutions (also includes imprisonment and other punishment reporting).
- Good business practise awareness training with business supply chain partners.
- Details of "well-being of employees" coverage including % of male and female workforce, permanent and other, covered by health insurance, accident insurance, maternity benefits, paternity benefits, and day care facilities.
- Workplace accessibility information.
- Retention of employees after parental leave – male and female and retention rates.
- Union representation rates – by worker category, male / female.
- Number of career development reviews – employees / workers; male / female.
- Numbers of accidents and injuries – worker / employee, lost time injury, fatalities, high consequence injuries.
- Participation in, and training on human rights – by worker category.

- Minimum wage payments – numbers by male / female; permanent / other.
- Remuneration paid – to board, key management personnel, employees, and workers.
- Complaints by employees with current status – sexual harassment; workplace discrimination; child labor; force / involuntary labor; wages; other human rights issues.

There then follows a list of topics to be discussed and disclosed related to disclosures around processes, policies, and procedures, which includes disclosure on areas of non-compliance. As can be seen, while there is a certain level of commonality, there are many areas that require a much deeper level of reporting. This list is a great example of potential "regulatory zeal" versus the value of the information to decision makers. Considering that *every* metric will typically require investment (both time and money) to collect and report, the organizational cost of suggested metrics must be compared to the value provided.

Europe already has in place guidelines[5] for non-financial reporting, which include areas such as:

- compliance with fundamentals of the International Labor Organization (ILO);
- human rights;
- diversity issues including race, gender, occupation etc.;
- employee demographics;
- trade union information and relationships;
- human capital "management," including restructuring, employability, career management, remuneration, training; and
- workplace health and safety.

---

[5] EU Guidelines on non-financial reporting (methodology for reporting non-financial information (2017/C 215/01)

The EU guidance gives specific examples of KPIs related to the above subjects. In 2021, the EU started work based on a new proposal for an extended and more comprehensive and updated approach to sustainability, which embraces the existing topics but also appears to cover the concepts of human capital as defined in the <IR> framework.

Most markets are looking at developing or updating guidelines, as well as mandatory requirements, in all these areas. Obviously, business has some level of "push back" related to both the volume of work required and the level of competitive disclosure being required. There will be a continuing dialogue as these "minimum" requirements develop, but organizations clearly need to prepare for greater human capital disclosure from the regulatory area.

In addition to the evolving statutory requirements, there are also well-established guidelines such as those from the GRI. These have been in place for several years, have been the subject of a great deal of discussion and evolution, and therefore suggest a good baseline to build from. They also reflect the experience of organizations that have practical experience in applying the guidelines and would therefore seem to provide a balanced view of what may be ahead.

The GRI framework is contained in a series of standards supported by sector-specific guidelines for application. The 100 series shown in Figure 3.3 contains the "universal standards" of thinking through and applying the reporting standards. Many of these suggested steps are similar to those in the <IR> framework and, to a degree, both of these sets of materials drive the thinking process that should be both incorporated into a management overview, and reflected in the governance section of Environmental, Social and Governance (ESG) reporting. The 200–400 series are topic-specific standards.

Series	Content
Foundation **GRI** **101**	The 100 series of Universal Standards that covers Reporting Principles, General Disclosures and Managements Approach. There are 3 documents in this series.
Economic **GRI** **200**	The 200 series of Topic Specific Standards that cover Economic aspects of sustainability reporting. There are 7 documents in this series.
Environmental **GRI** **300**	The 300 series Of Environmental Standards that cover disclosures relative to a broad base of environmental topics. There are 9 documents in this series.
Social **GRI** **400**	The 400 series of Social Standards that cover socially related aspects of sustainability reporting. There are 18 documents in this series.

Figure 3-3 The four series of GRI guidelines

Because the GRI guidelines pre-date the integrated reporting era, particularly the IIRC and the <IR> framework, the topic-specific approach groups items at a higher level – economic, environment and social – following the pre-existing corporate social responsibility structure.

While this in no way makes them less valuable as a resource, it does mean that there is not a clear correlation between human capital reporting and the GRI topics – so *extracting aspects that relate to human capital* is necessary. The list in Table 3.1 identifies suggested linkages. Note that the description given here is succinct; each guide should be studied in detail as the description is greatly expanded in the narrative within the standard.

Readers should look to organizations such as GRI and others, as the field of human capital metrics is developing rapidly.

Table 3.1 People-related topics from GRI guides

Human Capital Metrics

Guide	Topic	Description
200		**ECONOMIC TOPICS**
	201-1	Value distributed – employee wages by "appropriate" analysis
	201-3	Employee pension information
	202-1	Information related to pay / minimum wage by gender
	202-1	Numbers of locally hired senior management
	205-2	Anti-corruption awareness for employees (and others)
	205-3	Corruption terminations of employees
300		**ENVIRONMENT TOPICS**
400		**SOCIAL TOPICS**
	401-1	New hires and turnover by age group, gender, and region
	401-2	Benefits provided to full time employees
	401-2	Parental leave entitlement, use and return to work
	402-1	Notice (termination) time periods, union and non-union
	403-1	Information on Occupational Health and Safety management system (OHS)
	403-2	Hazard identification, risk assessment and incident investigation
	403-3	Occupational health services provided
	403-4	Worker participation, consultation, and communication on OHS
	403-5	Training on occupational health and safety
	403-6	Promotion of worker health
	403-7	Prevention and mitigation of occupational health and safety impacts linked by business relationships
	403-8	Workers covered by an occupational OHS management system
	403-9	Information on work-related injuries
	403-10	Information on work-related ill health
	404-1	Average hours of training / year / employee by gender / category
	404-2	Upgrading skills and employee transition assistance
	404-3	Performance and career development reviews
	405-1	Diversity of governance bodies and employees (gender / age / other – minority / vulnerable)
	405-2	Ratio of basic remuneration men to women by category / location

Guide	Topic	Description
	406-1	Incidents of discrimination and action taken
	407-1	Operations and suppliers in which right to freedom of association and collective bargaining may be at risk.
	408-1	Operations and suppliers at significant risk for incidents of child labor.
	409-1	Operations and suppliers at significant risk for incidents of forced or compulsory labor
	410-1	Security personnel trained in human rights policies or procedures
	411-1	Incidents of violations involving rights of indigenous peoples
	412-1	Operations that have been subject to human rights reviews or impact assessments
	412-2	Employee training on human rights policies or procedures
	412-3	Significant investment agreements and contracts that include human rights clauses or that underwent human rights screening

Clauses 413–419 in this topic (social) deal more with community relationships. As can be seen, there is a depth of reporting that exceeds the minimum currently being suggested by the existing or proposed SEC requirements.

While the GRI approach remains a discretionary one, it is already often used as a source of more prescriptive metrics within the more general model, such as integrated reporting using the <IR> framework (IIRC). However, what we see emerging is a core of metrics that suggests some level of "standard" coverage. The following list provides a suggested set of reporting topics:

- populations, diversity, and demographics;
- employee health and safety, accidents, safe workplace topics;
- recruitment and turnover information;
- compensation, benefits, and cost-related financial information;
- qualifications, career development, and training;
- employee engagement, culture, and labor relations;

- productivity and performance; and
- core areas of human rights compliance.

The existing and developing approaches all include several of these metrics. Some require information disclosed in narrative form, while others require metrics, or there is a combination of both. The approach to determining, developing, and calculating metrics is not always defined clearly or in a comparable way between different approaches, as illustrated in the comparison in Table 3.2. The major existing frameworks are given (columns), together with approximate equivalence of whether metrics (M), narrative (N) or both are required (or if the topic seems to be excluded). Is there an approach that might be comparable in approach, content, and calculation to the one being sought?

Table 3.2 Comparison of human topics in various frameworks

	WIDA	SEBI	EU	\<IR\>	GRI	ISO
Demographics / diversity	M/N	M/N	M/N	M	N	M
Health & safety	M	M/N	M/N	M	M/N	M
Human rights		M/N	M/N		M/N	
Recruitment	M		M/N	M	M	M
Turnover	M	M/N	M/N	M	M	M
Compensation & benefits	M/N	M/N	M/N	M	M/N	M
Engagement & culture	M/N	M/N		M/N		M/N
Labor relations		M/N	M/N	M/N	M/N	
Skills & competencies	M					
Training	M	M/N	M/N	M	M/N	M
Productivity				M		M
Costs				M		M

This then gives organizations a choice about potential starting points for external reporting. Before working on the metrics, it is important to think about issues such as scope, materiality, evaluation, consistency, and other critical decision points. Both the IIRC (the \<IR\> framework) and GRI have good information about the thinking process that needs to precede adoption of non-financial reporting information.

What about the final column – ISO? The International Standards Organization established a technical committee, TC 260, in 2011 with the purpose of developing management standards and guidelines on Human Resources Management; this work includes guidelines (and supporting technical specifications) on human capital metrics. The ISO defines management standards as: *"ISO standards that set out requirements or guidance to help organizations manage their policies and processes to achieve specific objectives."* The reader may be familiar with other management standards, such as ISO 9000 (Quality Management), ISO 14000 (Environmental Management), ISO 27000 (Information Technology), ISO 26000 (Corporate Social Responsibly), ISO 31000 (Risk Management), and ISO 45000 (Health and Safety).

Some people see little value in adopting standards; they see them as being far too prescriptive and bureaucratic. But, on the positive side, they reflect some level of consensus and, more importantly, define a standard approach, rather than a set of specific standards that *must* be used – that is up to the organization itself. Furthermore, the standard ensures that, if a particular metric is adopted, it is calculated and used consistently, allowing for comparison between organizations.

Management standards are built around conceptual frameworks and are developed by people experienced in the subject matter, who work together internationally and solicit ideas from key stakeholders to create documents that reflect leading thinking and practices at the time. Organizations can then use these documents as a foundation for how to develop their own approach.

In the early 1990s, the Chair of TC 176, the technical committee which developed the ISO 9000 series of Quality Management standards and guidelines was Reg Shaughnessy. In the early years (late 1980s–early 1990s), quality management was becoming a high priority (the standard was issued in 1987). This was also the time of Total Quality Management (TQM) and organizational excellence models such as The Baldrige Award, introduced in 1988. I was heavily involved in quality management at that time, and remember a conversation with Reg about the relevance and importance of international standards. He went to the flip chart (as was used in those days!) and quietly drew the picture represented in Figure 3.4.

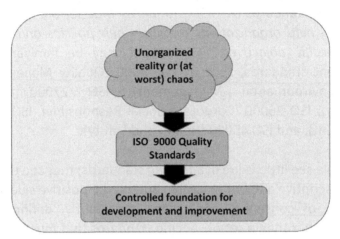

Figure 3.4 Seeking order using standards

In other words, the standard itself does not ensure good quality products or services, but it does provide a discipline and structure that can enable the development and implementation of an approach within each unique organization that, if developed, implemented, and maintained effectively, will significantly improve the probability and reliability of the organization to perform and meet its commitments.

In 2018, the ISO released one of many documents in the series of Human Resource Management standards, ISO 30414:2018 Human Resource Management *Guidelines for Internal and External Human Capital Reporting* (referred to hereafter as ISO 30414). The comparative chart shown earlier (Table 3.2), identifies key areas of human capital reporting that are common to many frameworks, ranging from occupational health and safety to productivity; the ISO standard provides a base for quantitative reporting on almost all the same categories. Missing are human rights and labor / management relations, and employee engagement and organizational culture, which is addressed using a qualitative rather than quantitative approach. In 2021, several new technical specifications were issued by ISO that supplement and expand ISO 30414; these include more metrics as well as expanded information on selection, application, calculation, and usage.

ISO 30414 contains a wealth of metrics; it also provides a framework for developing an approach to measuring human capital. While these are not discussed in depth here, there are also supporting technical specifications issued by the ISO that support and supplement ISO 30414, as listed in Table 3.3.

Table 3.3 List of ISO documents related to human capital (Nov 2021)

ISO 30414 Metrics Group	ISO Technical Specification Metrics Cluster
Compliance and ethics	ISO 30423:2021 Compliance and ethics
Costs	ISO 30427:2021 Cost
	ISO 30407:2017 Cost of Hire
Diversity	ISO 30415:2021 Diversity and inclusion
Leadership	ISO 30431:2021 Leadership
Organizational culture	ISO 24178:2021 Organizational Culture
Organizational health, safety and well being	ISO 24179:2020 Occupational health and safety
Productivity	ISO 30432:2021 Workforce productivity
Recruitment, mobility, and turnover	ISO 30430:2021 Recruitment
	ISO 30421:2021 Turnover and retention
	ISO 30410:2018 Impact of hire
	ISO 30411:2018 Quality of hire
Skills and capabilities	ISO 30428:2021 Skills and capabilities
Succession planning	ISO 30433:2021 Succession planning
Workforce availability	ISO 30425:2021 Workforce availability

The ISO 30414 guideline provides 58 metrics broken down into 11 categories. These are further divided into suggested metrics for internal and external reporting and those are then split to show recommended metrics for large, small or medium organizations.

While ISO 30414 is a guideline, and not a standard that can be certified by an ISO Registrar, there are organizations that will provide audit, verification, and certification services to provide evidence of adoption and implementation of these guidelines. This can create a strong discipline in the organization and demonstrate externally the commitment to a structured approach to human capital metrics.

It is recommended that readers purchase ISO 30414, as it contains much more information that can be provided here; for example, Table 3.4 lists the metrics included in the guidelines that are suggested as external reporting for large companies.

Table 3.4 ISO suggested topics for human capital metrics

ISO 30414 Metrics Group	Specific metrics – large organizations
Compliance and ethics	Number and type of grievances filed Number and type of concluded disciplinary action % Of employees who have completed training on compliance ad ethics
Costs	Total workforce costs

Diversity	Workforce diversity by:
	    a) age
	    b) gender
	    c) disability
	    d) Other indicators of diversity
	 Diversity of leadership team

Leadership	Leadership trust
Organizational culture	None for external
Organizational health, safety and wellbeing	Lost time injuries Number of occupational accidents Number of people killed during work

ISO 30414 Metrics Group	Specific metrics – large organizations
Productivity	EBIT per employee Revenue / turnover / employee Profit / employee Human capital ROI
Recruitment, mobility, and turnover	Average length of time to fill vacant positions Average length of time to fill critical business positions % Of positions filled internally % Of critical business positions filled internally Turnover rate (OUT)
Skills and capabilities	Total developing and training costs
Succession planning	None for external
Workforce availability	Number of employees Full time equivalents

It may be observed that two categories are not recommended here as external reporting – culture and succession planning; this decision will be further discussed in Chapter 6, "Choosing metrics for the model," which outlines why organizations might need to go beyond today's thinking – especially in these areas.

One of the key advantages of ISO 30414 is that it goes beyond the high-level metrics suggested by regulators such as the SEC, whose focus is typically on large, publicly traded organizations that form the minority of corporate organizations although attracting a high level of societal and investor interest.

The ISO provides several other metrics in addition to those listed above, which are shown Table 3.5. Note that ISO recommendations do in some cases suggest using the above indicators for both internal and external reporting, as well as for *all* sizes of organization.

Table 3.5 Topics for internal reporting

ISO 30414 Metrics Group	Specific metrics – all others
Compliance and ethics	Disputes referred to external parties
	Findings arising from these (audit, number, type)
Costs	External workforce costs
	Ratio of basic salary and remuneration
	Total costs of employment
	Cost per hire
	Recruitment cost
	Turnover costs
Diversity	All included in external
Leadership	Span of control
	Leadership development
Organizational culture	Engagement - satisfaction / commitment
	Retention rate
Organizational health, safety and well being	% Of employees who participated in H&S training
Productivity	All included in external
Recruitment, mobility, and turnover	Number of qualifies candidates / position
	Quality of hire
	Workforce capabilities (talent pool)
	% Of business positions that are critical
	% Of critical positions vacancies to all vacancies
	Internal mobility rate
	Employee bench strength
	Voluntary turnover without retirements
	Voluntary critical turnover rate
	Involuntary critical turnover rate
	Exit / turnover / leaving by reason

ISO 30414 Metrics Group	Specific metrics – all others
Skills and capabilities	% Of employees participating in learning and development
	Average formalized training hours / employee / year
	% Of employees by category who participated in formal training
	Workforce competency rate
Succession planning	Succession effectiveness rate
	Successor coverage rate
	Succession readiness rate, now
	Succession readiness rate, 1–3 years
	Succession readiness rate, 4–5 years
Workforce availability	Contingent workforce – independent contractors
	Contingent workforce – temporary workers
	Absenteeism

The specific metrics provide a rich starting point for developing preparedness for future external reporting, as well as voluntary compliance. Those pioneers and early adopters of metrics, including those who may have adopted the balanced scorecard and corporate dashboard approach, will probably already have some or many of these metrics in their portfolio.

Many of the current approaches to human capital metrics seem to be driven by building on tradition, that is using measures and indicators that have been used internally and which external users and regulators deem as "foundational." A review of the metrics laid out in this chapter might seem to indicate that they focus on certain dimensions of HR management and its place in corporate accountability to key stakeholders – in particular, investors and regulators. They appear to answer questions about:

- How much human capital is available?
- How much do we spend on human capital?
- Is our human capital reasonably stable?

- Does our employment match the make-up of society?
- Do we have a safe workplace?
- Do we invest in our people, both employees and leadership?
- What risks exist based on our ability to have the people we need?
- Are our people satisfied and engaged?
- What is the performance of some of our key HR processes?

This is all good information and adding this type of metric does increase visibility for external users. Inclusion of HR metrics demonstrates a willingness to recognize the value and strategic importance of the workforce in an organization's business model. It also goes some way to providing indicators on the "health" of the human capital as a core component of an organization's resilience and future sustainability in terms of operational capability.

The problem appears to be that, while some of these are good KPIs, they often provide no direct link to organizational value from an investor's perspective; nor do they address non-financial value other than the economic impact on society in terms the amount of money paid to the total workforce. There is no link to the role of human capital in the creation of intellectual capital, relationship capital or they key role human capital plays in the creation of "manufactured" capital in terms of intangible infrastructure. There is no link to the impact of the place of work on the workforce as members of society in areas such as stress and mental health. As a step on the journey, this foundation certainly moves human capital into a more visible role. But now the approach needs to be "changed up" to match future needs. Discussing what is needed is the topic of our next chapter, following which a framework for future human capital reporting will be suggested.

Existing metrics approaches – summary
• Many aspects of human capital reporting are driven by legislation – health and safety. These items can form a starting point.
• Organizations should look internally at what is currently available – possibly incorporated within a scorecard or dashboard.
• Several generic frameworks are already well-established – such as GRI (Global Reporting Initiative).
• Several new compliance areas are emerging from regulators – e.g., SEC, and other securities oversight organizations.
• Integrated Reporting <IR> has identified human capital as one of six key resources required for today's business model.
• Human capital metrics are needed because people are fast becoming the drivers of organizational capacity and capability.
• This new capacity and capability are driving value creation and generating intangible assets.
• The International Standards Organization (ISO) is active in developing human resource management standards and guidelines.
• Included in this ISO work is ISO 30414:2018 Guidance for developing human capital metrics; there are several supporting technical specifications available.
• GRI and <IR> provide guidance around the application and use of human capital metrics.
• Current development of the links between human capital and organizational value creation remains weak.

Starting point checklist
• What statutory human reporting requirements already exist under "people" legislation (e.g., workplace health and safety legislation)
• What human/ people reporting is already required for government statistical purposes (numbers of employees, vacations, work week, compensation etc.). Could any of this be used?
• Have standards or guidelines such as ISO been looked at as a source for metrics?
• What other existing reporting is already available e.g., training and development?
• Are any human capital "scorecard" or other reporting metrics already being used internally?
• Does HR have any existing metrics related to HR activities that are being used for activity / process monitoring?
• Are other organizational areas already using human capital metrics – e.g., legal or those creating supplemental "sustainability" or CSR reports?
• Does finance (or any other functional area) already provide human capital related reporting?

4 Why change is needed

So many of the metrics that are suggested, both in ISO 30414 and in other recommended frameworks related to human capital, are old; they have been in existence for over 30 years. While this does show a proven track record, it begs the question: Are they topical for the questions that need to be answered today? The answer is, probably not.

Where is the innovation that reflects the strategic importance of human capital to value creation? Where is the linkage between the financial value created and fully developing a workforce? Where is the link between the metrics and the transparency of risk related to enterprise resilience and sustainability? Do the metrics really provide users with the insight required to assess risk, performance, and the part that human capital plays in the market value of an organization?

Frankly, the existing metrics fall a bit short of expectations. This chapter will identify why current metrics are insufficient, and suggest some issues and thinking for an approach to human capital reporting that starts to build the bridge to real integration between all capitals.

Reporting of human capital is at a crossroads; while recognition of the importance of human capital is growing and with it the demand for greater understanding, the business world still seems to be attached to a functional view of reporting – in other words, human capital reporting is focused on what human resources are doing. Environmental, Social and Governance (ESG) reporting has gained recognition over the last decade or more, and it encourages a broadened approach to corporate accountability, where the heavy hitter remains climate change.

Human capital reporting remains under-developed, with many organizations populating the "people" part of their reports with existing, traditional HR data. There are several reasons for this:

- Many business models continue to be run as a collection of functional hierarchies.
- The only person who is expected to really understand "integration" is the CEO – because that is their job.
- Financial reporting remains a key measure of the business model "full system" performance, but financial accounts have a gaping hole in accounting for current models of value creation where cash is deployed to building intangible assets.
- Reporting – unless it is clearly linked to decision making – becomes a non-value added "overhead cost" to be avoided.
- Many users of corporate reporting are being overwhelmed by new metrics and narrative, and struggle with the quality, comparability and risk relevance of information being provided.
- Reconciling the changing role of business as a member of society remains a work in progress.

An earlier chapter outlined progress to date in changing corporate accountability and adapting to the need for more information, yet a much wider set of contextual changes is taking place that suggests a need to step back and re-think future reporting. These changes are not driven by new reporting models, seen as an evolution of the triple bottom line, corporate social responsibility, and climate change responses; they are related to fundamental changes in the world of business, suggesting that a totally new approach is needed. They are grouped into the following four categories, and will form a foundation for the new reporting approach being suggested here.

1. The changing social reality within which organizations operate.
2. The changing governance reality within which investors and senior managers operate.
3. The changing operational reality.
4. The changing leadership reality.

Each of these "pillars" of change is having a profound impact on the role, performance, behavior, and accountability of business.

4.1 The changing social reality for business

Changing social reality is addressed first because an organization's governance framework will reflect its responses to the environment within which it operates; this ensures that the way in which accountability, including reporting, is structured – in effect, its "license to operate[6]" – reflects the changing expectations of the society within which it operates.

The expectations of many people in society are that business must not only play by the rules, but it must also adhere to the unwritten rules that are part of cultural expectations. This increasing attention as to how business operates has been a constant behind the evolution of guidelines for good corporate governance, corporate social responsibility and now ESG reporting. The people that work for and with any organization are instrumental in demonstrating "corporate conduct;" those who lead it – boards and senior executives – must constantly monitor changing expectations and continually adapt their business model to remain within acceptable limits of society's expectations.

This "external monitoring" is not new for business: marketing's knowledge of changing customer expectations is a driver for growth; however,

---

[6] Social change is a constant, and business operates within a context determined by society – the framework of business is a social construct that has been created as a tool for economic activity. (Each) society sets the rules within which business operates; abiding by the rules is called the "license to operate."

increasingly, the public is looking not only at what an organization does, but also how it does it: how the organization behaves as a member of society. These shifts will continue to drive external accountability and reporting and the internal allocation of resources.

Globally, most countries have signed up to the SDGs (Social Development Goals) issued by the United Nations. This book is not the place for a discussion of ideologies or any other labels. What is suggested is that Member States have agreed to these societal gaols and the delivery of change that ensures their achievement will involve business. It has not traditionally been the "business of business" to meet social goals, but the world is changing. Milton Friedman spoke out strongly that *"the role of business is to make profit."* (If it is not illegal one can do it, and it is the role of government and regulators to build the desired social framework within which this can happen legally.) This challenge has not gone away, and the discussion is far from over about the role of ethical conduct – after all, courts and regulators cannot convict on unethical behavior, only illegal actions.

One example of this challenge is the issue of "fair" taxation. It is well known that organizations (and individuals) enhance cash flow and profitability by engaging in tax planning that often disadvantages certain countries in which they operate. This can contribute to challenges faced by the "disadvantaged" country in meeting social needs in its jurisdiction. Yet, in most cases, such tax planning is legal. While it may not be considered ethical by members of society, in few cases has it been proven to be illegal. (This is why actions by the recent G7 and G20 meetings of world leaders were needed to arrive at a minimum corporate tax within each jurisdiction in which a business operates; the reality is yet to be seen). In a highly competitive world, no business can afford not to take advantage of opportunities that its competitors may exploit; therefore, the expectation that companies will stop engaging in legal tax planning is unrealistic.

This is one example of a macro change that is taking place in the global arena in which business operates. Suggesting that a company should stop doing something for ethical reasons is a hard sell. However, if a gap opens up between the public's expectation of corporate behavior and its actions, and this starts to negatively impact the investors' value, say by depleting its brand value, then there is a linkage between societal behavior and shareholder value. As a final point on the tax issue, the recently issued GRI guideline (Guideline # 207 Tax) sets out reporting and disclosure suggestions for addressing this problem; however, on reading the guide, one can see that the drive is toward communication and legal compliance rather than voluntary ethical compliance and reporting.

What are the aspirations of these "high-level" Social Development Goals (SDG) that have been agreed to, and that nations are striving to adapt and change to meet? The full list is presented in Table 4.1.

Table 4-1 UN Social Development Goals (SDGs)

SDG	Title of the goal
1	No Poverty – end poverty in all its forms everywhere
2	Zero hunger – end hunger, achieve food security and improved nutrition and promote sustainable agriculture.
3	Good health and well-being – ensure healthy lives and promote well-being for all, at all ages.
4	Quality education – ensure inclusive and equitable education and promote lifelong learning opportunities for all.
5	Gender equality – achieve gender equality and empower all women and girls.
6	Clean water and sanitation – ensure availability and sustainable management of water and sanitation for all.
7	Affordable and clean energy – ensure access to affordable, reliable, sustainable, and modern energy for all.
8	Decent work and economic growth – promote sustained, inclusive, and sustainable economic growth, full and productive employment, and decent work for all.

SDG	Title of the goal
9	Industry, innovation, and infrastructure – build resilient infrastructure and sustainable industrialization and foster innovation.
10	Reduced inequalities – reduce inequality within and among countries.
11	Sustainable cities and communities – make cities and human settlements inclusive, safe, resilient, and sustainable.
12	Responsible consumption and production – ensure sustainable consumption and production patterns.
13	Climate action – take urgent action to combat climate change and its impacts.
14	Life below water – conserve and sustainably use the oceans, seas, and marine resources for sustainable development.
15	Life on land – protect, restore, and promote sustainable use of terrestrial ecosystems, sustainably manage forests, combat desertification, and halt and reverse land degradation and halt biodiversity loss.
16	Peace, justice, and strong institutions – promote peaceful and inclusive societies for sustainable development, provide access to justice for all and build effective, accountable, and inclusive institutions at all levels.
17	Partnerships for the goals – strengthen the means of implementation and revitalize the global partnership for sustainable development.

This book does not suggest that business will be accountable, or even responsible for the achievement of these goals. However, there is a significant link with human capital and, as such, the impact that any organization's conduct has on people's lives will be woven into future strategy – whether through changing compliance, public expectations or changing roles within the economic system. How people behave and how the business is seen to behave will increasingly drive what type of reporting is required.

4.2   The changing governance reality

As organizations adapt to both social change and progress, their structures, models, and frameworks must all be modified to align with current reality. This is a core responsibility of both the board and the CEO, who, through the process of strategic planning, will ensure clarity of purpose together with a framework for execution. A reflection of this changing purpose is illustrated by the 2019 statement by the Business Round Table[7] in a press release entitled *Business Roundtable Redefines the Purpose of a Corporation to Promote 'An Economy That Serves All Americans,'* announcing their shift in direction:

> *WASHINGTON – Business Roundtable today announced the release of a new Statement on the Purpose of a Corporation signed by 181 CEOs who commit to lead their companies for the benefit of all stakeholders – customers, employees, suppliers, communities, and shareholders.*
>
> *Since 1978, Business Roundtable has periodically issued Principles of Corporate Governance. Each version of the document issued since 1997 has endorsed principles of shareholder primacy – that corporations exist principally to serve shareholders. With today's announcement, the new Statement supersedes previous statements and outlines a modern standard for corporate responsibility.*
>
> *"The American dream is alive, but fraying," said Jamie Dimon, Chairman and CEO of JPMorgan Chase & Co. and Chairman of Business Roundtable. "*Major employers are investing in their workers and communities because they know it is the only way to be successful over the long term. These modernized principles reflect the business community's unwavering commitment to continue to push for an economy that serves all Americans."

---

[7] https://www.businessroundtable.org/business-roundtable-redefines-the-purpose-of-a-corporation-to-promote-an-economy-that-serves-all-americans

> "This new statement better reflects the way corporations can and should operate today," *added Alex Gorsky, Chairman of the Board and Chief Executive Officer of Johnson & Johnson and Chair of the Business Roundtable Corporate Governance Committee.* "It affirms the essential role corporations can play in improving our society when CEOs are truly committed to meeting the needs of all stakeholders."

This represents a profound shift, especially as it reflects both the changing social realities and the progress made on alternative reporting frameworks, particularly the <IR> structure. The embracing of stakeholders by the Business Roundtable clearly supports the broadened base of capital resources, as indicated in Figure 4.1.

Financial capital	Social and relationship capital
Natural capital	Manufactured capital
Human capital	Intellectual capital

Figure 4.1 The six resource capitals of integrated thinking

What is important here is the recognition that value creation now involves much more than financial capital. This shift in value creation is driving both new governance models as well as vastly different approaches to resource allocation and therefore have significant implications on reporting and accountability.

4.2.1 The implications for traditional financial reporting

The development of the concept of six capitals has evolved over time and reflects a systemic change from a world of tangible assets to one of "intangibles." Financial capital and cash flow continue to be the life blood of an organization. Investors are paid in cash dividends and interest; investors contribute cash as a core component of any start up – but the change in the use of cash has become important. Management now direct vast amounts of cash to building business models based on the six capitals, many of which still rely initially on financial capital. What has changed is that the cash is just used differently. A large part of the cash now flows to human capital and human capital is the creator of many of the other intangible capitals.

Because of this change in the use of cash, accountability and reporting need to change, and nowhere is this more important than in human capital. People are probably *the* major consumer of cash for most organizations, but what has changed is that much of the money that is paid as "payroll and benefits" is no longer applied to pay for the creation of current products and services; rather, it goes to create and sustain an intangible "infrastructure" that ensures enterprise sustainability, continuity and the resilience of the business value creation model.

This shift has major implications for external reporting as well as internal decision making. The workforce has shifted from providing labor to providing brain power. This shift is profound for the accounting profession and for users of financial information; it not only affects the way financial information is presented (and highlights the current inadequacy of understanding intangibles), it also undermines the whole foundation of accounting.

While accounting and financial reporting are considered well-established, it is evident that significant changes have taken place, as the underlying business models have evolved. Understanding the evolution of financial reporting is useful in establishing the need for further changes to reflect the current business reality, especially in the evolution of intangibles and, in particular, the financial implications of human capital.

Financial information in recorded form will have started as lists of transactions, and this further evolved when Friar Luca Bartolomeo de Pacioli (1446–1517) improved the recording of transactions through the creation of double-entry bookkeeping, which is still the foundation for recording accounting transactions today. The original financial statement was a balance sheet that showed assets, liabilities, and net worth. As assets and liabilities changed, net worth also changed; for many years, this was enough information for both investors and decision makers.

However, in the 18th century, the need for greater understanding of the changes in "net worth" or "equity" developed, and the income statement was created to show all the transactions involved, leading to the creation of a statement of profit or loss – addition to or depletion of an investor's equity or worth. Shareholders and other investors started to question what had happened to the money when their net worth changed. By the 20th century, the need for a reconciliation between cash and non-cash transactions was recognised, and the cash flow statement started to become important. (It may be worth noting that cash flow became increasingly important in resource companies, as their key "asset" was often intangible, being natural capital.)

Prior to the Great Depression that took place mostly during the 1930s, there were few rules that had to be adhered to in creating financial statements; however, afterwards (and due to the stock market crash in 1929 that started it), political pressure led to the creation of more robust standard setting in many countries. In the USA, the SEC was established, which, in turn, led to the creation, in 1973, of the Financial Accounting Standards Board (FASB). In the UK, Canada, and many other industrialized countries, similar organizations were set up. While the types of financial statements were well-established by the 20th century, the method of record keeping and presenting information was constantly changing.

This brings us to the post-industrial era, in which the most significant change to the economic model – the emergence of intangibles as the drivers of value creation – is taking place. Table 4.2 demonstrates the gap between traditional financial accounting – the "net worth" – of the five well-known knowledge-based organizations, referred to collectively as

FAANG[8], and the value as determined by the marketplace (what it costs to invest).

While comparing anything to market values one has to accept that the market may go up or down depending on general economic conditions (real and perceived), and does not always represent an accurate number of true value; however, over time, there does appear to be a significant growing gap between what the accounting records (used for financial reporting) suggest an organization's net worth is and the market value. Investors, shareholders, and decision makers might, once again, wonder where their money went.

Table 4.2 Market value of the "FAANG" stocks (in billion $)

Jan 1st 2020	Market Value	Brand Value	Book Value	Other Intangibles	Brand Value	Book Value	Other Intangibles
Facebook	$647,840	$79,804	$105,306	$462,730	12.3%	16.3%	71.4%
Apple	$1,581,000	$234,241	$78,423	$1,268,336	14.8%	5.0%	80.2%
Amazon	$1,376,000	$220,791	$65,368	$1,089,841	16.0%	4.8%	79.2%
Netflix	$200,680	$22,945	$9,334	$168,401	11.4%	4.7%	83.9%
Google (+)	$967,990	$167,713	$203,659	$596,618	17.3%	21.0%	61.6%
	$4,773,510	$725,494	$462,089	$3,585,927	15.2%	9.7%	75.1%

It should be stressed that the numbers in Table 4.2 reflect *billions of dollars*! Apple's market value at the beginning of 2020 was about $1.6 trillion (and since then it has risen to more than $2 trillion); yet its accounts show a book value – i.e., assets less liabilities = net worth (shareholders equity) of only $78 billion. In other words, the financial statements suggest that the accounting (book) value is only 5% of what investors are willing to pay for the "system" and what it generates in earnings and appreciation. A large part of this "system" is the capability of the workforce. (For more

---

[8] FAANG: Facebook, Amazon, Apple, Netflix, and Google, –although at the time of writing two have changed their names – Facebook to Meta and Google to Alphabet!

on the whole problem of accounting values and tracking of intangibles, the reader is referred to my book, *How Accountants Lost their Balance*.[9])

The problem of the widening gap between accounting book value and market value has been growing for many years – mainly as a result of the shift to an intangible economy, in which human capital and the value of "people" play a significant role.

This was discussed earlier. In 2000, book value had already declined, and represented only about 25% of total market value. Ocean Tomo has been charting these changes for several decades (as was seen earlier in Figure 3); their chart (Figure 4.2) shows how intangible assets have grown from 17% of organizational value in 1975 to 90% by 2020.

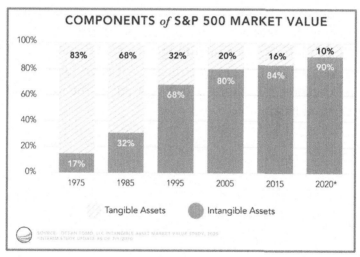

Figure 4.2 Intangibles as a percentage of investors' value / risk. Source: Ocean Tomo LLC

While an investor may be interested in the sustainability of their investment, financial reporting can only explain the book value. The gap

---

[9] Shepherd, Nick, *How Accountants Lost their Balance: How the profession has drifted away from reality and must adapt to an intangible world*, 2021, Eduvision Inc. available from Amazon (worldwide – paperback / Kindle).

created by intangibles represents the resources and capabilities that management has invested in to create a functioning business model – yet there is no reporting of where this money went. More importantly for the investor, there is no risk assessment as to whether these intangible investments are being sustained and nurtured, and what impact their "health" has on sustainable operational capability. Intangibles, including human capital investments, form a major part of this gap. For effective reporting of human capital in the future, there must be some level of linkage between economic value, financial capital, and non-financial capital. Current approaches are not solving this issue.

As these shifts have been taking place, traditional financially focused reporting (and audits) is providing less and less visibility to both decision makers and investors, who face uncertainty in understanding how this focus on intangibles is affecting their risk and the sustainability and resilience of their investment. Over the years, management has directed billions of dollars into creating an intangible infrastructure, including their workforce – but where is this investment? If it is an "asset", where is it? Has it been depleted? Is there a risk related to the sustainability and capability of human capital?

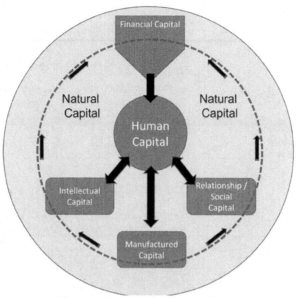

Figure 4.3 Human capital as the driver of other intangibles

As shown in Figure 4.3, human capital can be seen as the driver of other intangibles. The link between financial capital and human capital *must* be a part of future reporting, as must the outcome of human capital in terms of the other intangible capitals. Future reporting must also answer the questions" Where did the money go? and Is the investment still optimized? It also needs to give information on how much of the organization's value is hidden away in the workforce.

Some evolutionary thinking is taking place around the concept of the "hidden balance sheet." After all, when value was synonymous with the financial records, the balance sheet informed investors and management about what their net worth was made up of (or at least about 90% of it).

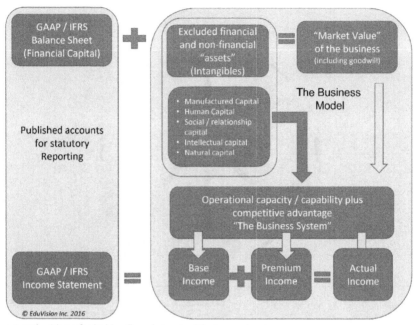

Figure 4.4 The idea of a hidden "market value" balance sheet

Could some type of balance sheet concept be developed to explain the gap? The graphic in Figure 4.4 demonstrates how the reconciliation between accounting (book) value and market value might be explained by the intangibles – the other capitals that have been invested in.

Using this idea, traditional financial reporting remains the same, but some type of supplemental reporting could explain the gap between book and market value by trying to assign financial "value" to intangibles, for example, by means of the brand or market value. In the following example, taken from the earlier table of the FAANG stocks, Amazon had a market value of $1.376 trillion, but of this only 4.8% was represented by the book value, i.e., the amount included in traditional financial reporting; the other 95.2% reflects what could have been in the hidden balance sheet. Using these numbers, we can see that, at the time, the market estimate of the brand (which might be considered a representation of some level of its social and relationship capital) explained 16.0%, leaving 79.2% of "something else." Part of this is the amount invested in human capital in terms of capability for innovation, creativity, and key relationship developments (see Table 4.3 for an example).

Table 4.3 The hidden impact of human capital value at Amazon (Jan 1, 2020)

Jan 1st 2020	Market Value	Brand Value	Book Value	Other Intangibles	Brand Value	Book Value	Other Intangibles
Amazon	$1,376,000	$220,791	$65,368	$1,089,841	16.0%	4.8%	79.2%

Given the value of an organization in the market and the gap between the market and book values, it might be tempting to try and develop a financial value for the underlying component parts. The assumption might be that if financial values could be calculated for underlying intangibles, this could go some way toward explaining the gap in value. Could the workforce be valued like an asset? Certain organizations, such as Accountants for Sustainability (A4S), are trying to do this, to determine workforce value, and have published case studies of their approaches. However, as stated in the Golden Rule below, there are reasons why this exercise will not provide a solution:

THE GOLDEN RULE
- The organization as an <u>integrated whole</u> has a financial value.
- The component parts, such as human capital contribute to value creation but cannot be disaggregated as a defined element of system value.

To explain this golden rule – related to human capital, in particular: People are not owned by an organization but are contractually acquired as an external service. While each person has a market value individually, especially those with skills that are in demand, their value within an organization depends heavily on both the work environment (to be discussed later) and the "enablers" that they depend on. This was why some of the most important questions in the survey contained in Buckingham and Coffman's book[10] (note the original version of the book is now out of print - but may still be available in some stores) included issues related to:

- Understanding PUROSE and how it relates to my own job.
- Having a workplace / workspace that provides what I need to "do a good job."

Secondly, as was ably explained in the work of Eli Goldratt[11] (which should still be standard business reading!), any change in input resources, even capital equipment, changes the performance of the total system. The impact can only be assessed in terms of total system performance.

Organizational value also has another meaning outside financial value; if one looks at the traditional financial definitions, such as given on the website investopedia[12], there is a good explanation of all the different financial values. But there are other definitions of value that are becoming increasingly important, especially in a knowledge economy. Organizations already have an economic value to society in terms of providing necessary goods or services, creating employment, paying taxes, etc. Many of these economic values can be linked to financial metrics as key indicators.

Ultimate organizational performance is measured in outcomes – such as profitability and market value – but the "system" generates other important outcomes that need to be evaluated and measured. A starting point might be to take another look at the UN SDGs discussed earlier and determine whether the business system is creating positive (or negative)

---

[10] Buckingham, Marcus, and Coffman, Curt, *First, break all the rules*, 1999, Gallup / Simon & Schuster.
[11] Goldratt, Eli, *Theory of Constraints*, 1999, North River Press; and Goldratt, Eli., *The Goal*, 1982 (Revised 2012), North River Press.
[12] https://www.investopedia.com/terms/v/value.asp

outcomes in these areas. The outcome of employing people will contribute to both financial and non-financial outcomes.

For human capital reporting, non-financial outcomes must also be considered because these can have a negative or positive impact on the organization, either directly or indirectly. Some examples of these other outcomes are given below:

- Creation of intellectual capital (some of which can have a financial value in the marketplace).
- Creation of relationship / social capital leading to items such as brand value and reputation, but also impacting quality and ease of hiring.
- Creation of manufactured capital – tangible (that might have a financial value), but also intangible such as codified processes and procedures.
- Increase in intellectual / human capital through internal development, increasing internal bench strength and promotions.
- Impact on societal / community sustainability through investing in employees' learning and development.
- Impact on society through creating an effective culture that minimizes accident rates but also minimizes stress and mental health issues, that, if not achieved results in negative "externality" impact on the community (health care, policing, social services).
- Impact on human capital (non-financial) value in terms of retention rates leading to (non-financial) value of the workforce.
- Impact on intellectual capital in terms of the value of the "model for innovation" that is created through a collaborative and cooperative culture.

If one considers the monetization of these non-financial outcomes, they are, to a great degree, the aspects of the "system capability" that is created and which forms part of the financial value of the whole system. If one looks at each item, almost all of these capabilities would be assessed as a "system capability" in terms of the attractiveness of an investment, or a merger / acquisition. Thus, under US accounting rules, certain "acquired intangibles" can be added to an organization's balance sheets as an asset, because at that point they have been monetized.

These capabilities represent the intangible values of the system as a whole. They cannot be disaggregated, and each given an accurate value (although some might be easier to convert than others), but the ability to manage and sustain these capabilities depends heavily on the integrity of the system. Failure is often seen after a merger or acquisition when the system is first disaggregated and then re-integrated, and the assessment is that the premium paid by the buyer for these capabilities (goodwill), has been impaired. The integrity of the system has been lost and, because of this, the financial value has been depleted. Again, a large part of the value is the value of the workforce.

Thus, value needs to be thought of as a much wider issue than financial representation. What is needed is both a recognition and reporting of non-financial outcomes, and an assessment of these non-financial outcomes and the performance and sustainability of the business model. Only through this connection can investors and others begin to understand the risks and impacts of management decision making and performance. This thinking is a *core* part of the governance in ESG performance, as well as a critical aspect of assessing materiality when deciding what should be reported.

To fill this void, especially given the financial impact of people on the organization's performance, accounting has become involved and appears to be using traditional accounting and financial reporting tools to complement HR numbers. The result is actions such as creating a "value" for the workforce, as though it were an asset on the balance sheet. Additionally, efforts have been made to develop Return on Investment (ROI) numbers for human capital, to link the effectiveness of HR strategies to profitability. I believe that both these approaches are well-intentioned but ultimately flawed, even if one considers them only as key indicators.

Human capital – people – only have a value when they become part of the system which is what produces the ultimate organizational performance. There are many other factors within the system that enable their level of performance. One can have the smartest, best-qualified people on the payroll, but if they do not have the equipment and materials needed to do their job or are not surrounded and led by a culture that enables and optimizes their potential, then the organization will not optimize its total capability.

What is needed is a hybrid approach, that builds on what already exists but takes a new approach to understanding and reporting human capital or the role of people in organizational success. This starts with understanding the problem before adopting a solution and that is where we will go next.

4.2.2 The changing concept of value and value creation

The financial shift described above has had profound impacts on how organizations create "value" and build their business models. While business is not all about financial value, its ultimate performance has historically been judged in these terms. Any business also needs cash to "prime the pump" and to fund the initial development of any "system capability." More money is then needed to scale up these capabilities – so investor cash and financial reporting will always remain important.

For the investor, market value of the company is a great aggregate measure of how well management has brought together all the resources needed in their business model, and as a result, how much someone would pay for the underlying business model or "system" together with its earnings capability.

The traditional business model has not changed, as shown by the core <IR> business model in Figure 4.5; however, the content of the "input" has shifted significantly. "operationalizing" a business involves:

- acquiring ownership or access to **inputs** (the resources required for the business model, a key part of which is human capital);
- developing operational processes that involve **activities** and tasks, as well as managing projects (the "operationalizing" of the resources);
- **outputs** (the results created from the various operational stages); and, ultimately, assuming everything works as planned, delivering the desired
- **outcomes** (the results created in terms of the "system" as a whole).

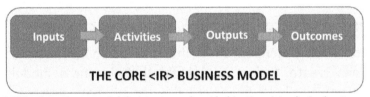

Figure 4.5 The four-stage model that turns goals and objectives into desired outcomes

The outcome of the system as a whole has traditionally been focused primarily on the single common denominator of profit, although other metrics – some demonstrated by Kaplan and Norton in their work on the scorecard – would include customer satisfaction and employee learning and growth. But this picture has changed, and the business system now has identified inputs and outputs that are non-financial – as can be seen in Figure 4.6.

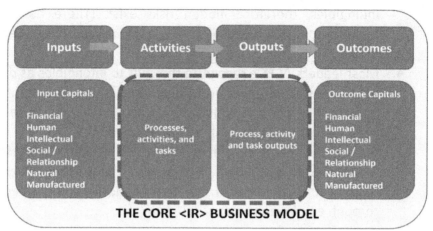

Figure 4.6 The core <IR> business model showing the six capitals

From a governance perspective, all six capitals should now be part of reporting related to the business model and its operations and risks. The implication for human capital is significant – a large portion of investors' cash flow is being assigned to people, for training and development, leadership development, team development, problem solving, health, safety and many others; additionally, human capital is the main creator of relationships, intellectual capital and "codified" manufactured capital (which, in an intangible world, is represented by processes, systems, procedures – in effect the intangible infrastructure).

Profitability is a great measure again of the aggregated system performance – a snapshot of short-term performance. In the previous section, it was clearly demonstrated that the market value of today's organization has become "the" measure of financial value. There are some problems here, though, that must be addressed and will have an impact on human capital reporting:

- The market financial value is underpinned by a system (business model) which is heavily reliant on intangibles. Current reporting and audits do not inform investors of the health of these

- intangibles, therefore hidden risks exist. (There have been organizations that have failed after a "clean" audit, e.g., Carillion in the UK.)
- Most leaders / CEOs recognize the shift to intangibles as drivers of business activity and are directing massive amounts of cash into creating and sustaining these capabilities; yet there is no visibility to investors or others of this activity.
- One of the major consumers of intangible investment is the workforce. Human capital is costly to acquire, deploy and sustain; it also creates a negative financial impact when lost through employee turnover.

This shift towards recognition of the changing importance of inputs and outcomes requires that boards and management take a different view of materiality in terms of importance and risk assessment, but also of how operations are approached and managed. Much of the existing reporting on human resources focuses on operational performance using metrics such as revenue, sales, turnover per employee, net profit of EBIT / employee, and HC-ROI.

What is needed instead is an approach to integrated reporting, in which all the operational aspects of the six capitals are considered. This has significant implications for human capital: while people, as part of the system, contribute to the generation of financial outcomes, they also impact other capitals which need to be measured. This is a core task of integrated reporting, and human capital metrics need to be a central component.

4.3   The changing operational reality – the shift to multiple capitals

As changes to reporting have occurred, reflecting changing realities for management, investors, regulators, and others (both internally, with tools like the balanced scorecard or corporate dashboard, and externally, through the triple bottom line, CSR, GRI guidelines, SASB and others), two parallel approaches to external reporting started to evolve. Although the need for integration was addressed through the formation of the IIRC in 2012, and then by the IIRC guidelines (the six capitals together with a concept of integrating financial and non-financial reporting), real integration of business performance reporting has been slow.

While multi-faceted reporting using the six capitals, focusing on natural capital in particular, has made significant progress, the relationship between and among the capitals remains to be understood and crystallized. The reporting of financial performance has remained traditional, with few clear links to the other developing capitals. This has led to a growing concern about the myriad of models, lack of comparability, and sheer volume of data being published (as an example, the H2020 Human Resources report for Deutsche Bank runs to 106 pages, and while the scope is broader than some of the minimum standards and guidelines set out, it is still a lot of information for *one* of the six capitals). There is also limited linkage between human capital and value creation.

By 2021, this evolution of demand for enhanced reporting reached a point of consolidation and focus. When the IIRC issued its original guidelines with the six capitals concept in 2013, it was hoped that these would be universally adopted by 2020, but this did not happen. However, the cost and complexity of reporting did bring together many of the key players to collaborate on moving forward. The following statement was released in late 2020:

> *"...[F]ive framework- and standard-setting institutions of international significance, CDP, the Climate Disclosure Standards Board (CDSB), the Global Reporting Initiative (GRI), the International Integrated Reporting Council (IIRC) and the Sustainability Accounting Standards Board (SASB), have co-published a shared vision of the elements necessary for more comprehensive corporate reporting and a joint statement of intent to drive towards this goal – by working together and by each committing to engage with key actors, including IOSCO and the IFRS, the European*

> *Commission, and the World Economic Forum's International Business Council."*

The International Federation of Accountants (IFAC) also issued a joint press release with the IIRC in early 2021, indicating agreement to work together to develop approaches for "assurance" of integrated reports – a role that accountants have held globally for financial reporting for many years:

> *To help meet this demand (for added assurance), and to increase confidence in integrated reporting, the International Federation of Accountants (IFAC) and the International Integrated Reporting Council (IIRC) today, 26 February 2021, are launching a new joint initiative, Accelerating Integrated Reporting Assurance in the Public Interest.*

It should be recognized that this agreement focuses on "audit and assurance" and does nothing to address the continuing inability of financial reporting to shine light on the major amounts of financial resources that are directed at hiring, managing, leading, developing, and sustaining the workforce.

Accounting seems to continue to believe that most of the money spent on the workforce is a "period expense" with no long-term value and, therefore, it can be written off as incurred. This depletes shareholders' equity and accounting value, yet, in reality, *grows* the value of the organization. For shareholders, there is no answer to the questions, Where did my money go? or Is management taking care of the major investments we have committed to workforce development?

The involvement of financial capital and accounting in human capital metrics is important. Solutions may not come from looking to change accounting standards but there must be some bridge between the impact of financial capital and the important role that "funding people" plays in developing intangible capability, which drives the value stream and the intangibles-based business model.

Figure 4.7 shows the integrated nature of financial capital, human capital among others.

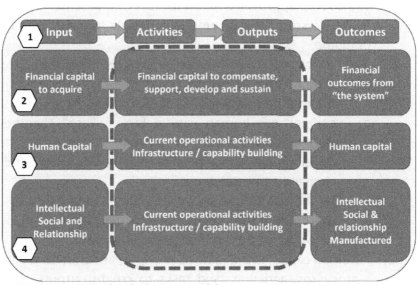

Figure 4.7 Human capital within the business model

Stream 1 reflects the basic business model of input, activity, outputs, and outcomes, while Stream 2 shows financial capital as the input that is converted to human capital, which then creates the "organization-level" system outputs and outcomes. In Stream 3, it can be seen that human capital brings intellectual capital with it as an input, and this is then converted into "intangible infrastructure," providing the organizational operating capability. Finally, Stream 4 reflects that human capital also brings with it, as an input, key relationships both internal and external. None of this can happen without financial capital being converted into human capital.

Understanding, monitoring, and measuring human capital *only* as an input that creates financial outputs and outcomes is no longer adequate.

The following list illustrates the complexity of integrated reporting using human capital as an example. Looking at each of the four streams in the above business model, we can see that:

1. The overall approach of the business model remains unchanged at the "system" level, comprising inputs, process, outputs, and outcome.
2. Financial capital (one of the six capitals) is still required to:
    a. acquire human capital (i.e., investment to cover hiring, orientation / onboarding, basic training etc.);
    b. compensate human capital for its "use" together with ongoing investment to sustain it, such as training, development, coaching, health care, safety etc.; and is also changed as an outcome
    c. by the use of human capital, plus all the other resources used during the processes, activities, and tasks (i.e., profit or loss as well as changed market value).
3. Human capital is available as an input, and is utilized within the processes, activities, and tasks to create outputs, as well as outcomes, which include the state / condition of the workforce "after the process has been completed." These outcomes relate to the resulting "state" of human capital as a result of its utilization; this might include physical and mental health, experience, upgrades in training among others.
4. Other capitals are also available to, and may be utilized by, the application of human capital, or are intrinsic to human capital itself. As an example, intellectual capital can be codified and become intellectual property (IP), or it can be tacit, in which case it is "in the head" of the individual member(s) of the workforce. Other capitals are also used by human capital as part of the process activity, e.g., manufactured capital (such as computers). Additionally, other capitals are created as an outcome of human capital activity – building relationships, growing brand values, creating more intellectual property, etc.

This illustrates the breadth of reporting needed if true integration among the capitals is to be realized. For external users, this could be a daunting task and begs the question: Which indicators are the critical few? This discussion *must* take place at the governance level and depicts the criticality among and between the six capitals in terms of risk management and the ability to sustain a resilient and stable value creation system.

To further emphasize the impending need for change in reporting, the UK Government recently issued a consultative paper on the approach to audits that includes the phrase: *"…audits (need) to extend beyond financial results, looking at wider performance and ESG targets."*

The quality of HR metrics, as a core aspect of ESG reporting – especially governance (G) – has reached a tipping point. The approach to governance relative to the functioning of the business model must focus on the effective management of *all* resources to create a system capable of both operational effectiveness and sustainable capability. The thinking of profit maximization must give way to governance that optimizes the use and outcomes of all capitals to ensure system integrity. Not doing so is creating systemic risk.

All six capitals are critical for sustainability and there is a risk element to the whole system from each of the component parts. While financial risk remains important, to this must be added the (till now) hidden quality and health of the other capitals required for a healthy integrated system. This must be the goal of effective integrated reporting. The graphic in Figure 4.8 depicts the thinking that might be used to assess a system that is in balance: the whole system is being optimized to ensure sustainability.

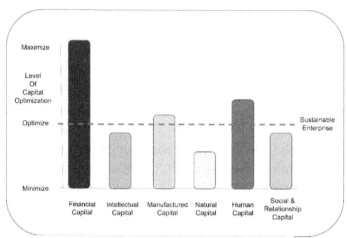

Figure 4.8 The challenge of optimizing all capitals

This would result in management having to make continuing trade-offs between the different capitals. For example, the decision may be whether to avoid layoffs to keep the core, knowledgeable workforce and so avoid re-training and start-up costs *or* to lay off the workforce to minimize negative financial impacts. Financial reporting tends to reward the layoff option: the "value" of a trained workforce is not shown as an investment or reported, nor are the costs related to either the loss of investment that is created when a layoff occurs, or re-training after layoff; they are just seen as overall training costs – as current metrics disclose. Additionally, the impact on motivation and underlying intellectual capital is never revealed. Given current approaches, financial capital tends to be maximized rather than optimized, hiding the underlying impact of the "invisible" other capitals.

At this point, it might be worth remembering the old phrase, "People are our most important asset." In a knowledge economy, human capital consumes the most significant portion of financial capital, plays a key role in ongoing performance, and is the creator of several of the other capitals in terms of outcomes.

4.4 The changing leadership reality

The previous section discussed the complexity of integration and outlined the critical role that human capital plays in an integrated business system. One of the underlying changes that has been taking place is the role of leadership as it applies to human capital. Leadership is both a quality of, and a part of the investment in, human capital.

Much of the current reporting of human capital is focused on the competencies, skills, and capabilities of the workforce, and activities relative to training and development, for example; but human capital reporting in a knowledge or intangible economy must address both the "stock" of human capital (i.e., the experience, qualifications and other capabilities of the workforce), and the health and quality of the work environment as a "crucible" within which talented people can perform at their highest level.

There are unique challenges in reporting on human resources. First, the impact of people permeates every aspect of an organization's activity – so what to report? Second, people are unique because they possess a complex combination of personalities that have grown and adapted to their surroundings. They may have also become educated to some level, with skills sets that may match organizational needs. However, their willingness to fully engage these skill sets for the benefit of an organization will often depend on emotional responses to how they are, or perceive they are, treated by others – especially supervision and leadership.

People are also not owned by the organization they work for, so they cannot be considered "assets" in the traditional (financial) sense. In effect, they "rent out" their services, seeking a fair exchange between what they provide and the rewards that they receive. This is in part why the work environment becomes so critical – if it fails to both attract and retain people, they can leave.

Most HR professionals know that people often cite "better pay" as a reason for leaving but, in many cases, especially for skilled employees, a better work environment is the attraction. Human capital reporting must go beyond reporting on the organization's "talent pool," HR process performance and investments in training and development, to address the work climate that "energizes" (or empowers and engages) the workforce.

If one looks at current suggestions for human capital reporting, areas such as turnover / retention are included, as well as indicators that may suggest what the "quality" of the workplace is; these include information about terminations, grievances, pay equity, health and safety, diversity and others. However, many of these are metrics required for statutory reporting purposes and only give limited view of the "health" of the workplace.

While turnover might be considered an important outcome metric, strategically there are also important additional outcomes – such as supporting behavioral aspects of reputation and brand – with customers seeing the organization's employees as "helpful" and "willing to go the extra mile to solve problems." Also, aspects that would help recruitment, such as becoming a preferred employer have become strategically important in the acquisition of talent.

The chart in Figure 4.9 depicts the required combination of skills and engagement: the **core assets** related to the input of human capital, i.e., knowledge, experience, etc., *plus* the ability of leadership to **engage the workforce** to optimize the potential. Only through the combination of both these aspects of human capital, will an organization **create value**, and build its competitive advantage. This is a *key* aspect of workforce value, representing a major shift forward in human capital metrics. It breaks out from the composite organizational effectiveness measures the impact of a motivating workplace.

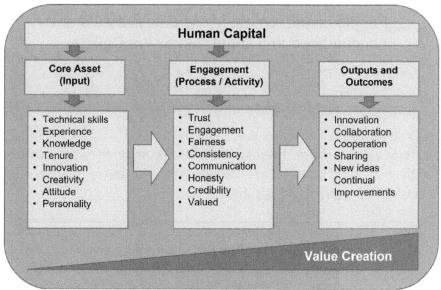

Figure 4.9 Criticality of talent plus healthy workplace culture

While the core asset aspect of human capital is the availability of the skills, knowledge, and experience necessary to execute the required activities, these are passive metrics; having a highly skilled workforce is of little value if the capabilities are not being fully optimized operationally. The environment within which the work takes place is often more important in creating and sustaining a competitive advantage than having the skills. This is what enables the optimum performance to be gained from the workforce.

Engagement also requires investment, both to build a positive and supportive environment and to sustain it. Investors and others are at risk if reporting addresses only the core capabilities of the workforce and ignores the work environment. Value creation, in terms of both organizational performance and market value, comes from the *combination* of talent and environment (i.e., culture). So, whatever HR metrics are developed and reported, there must be both "talent" aspect *and* a "culture" aspect, as illustrated by Figure 4.10.

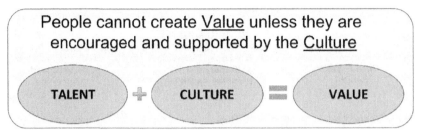

Figure 4-10 Value creation through people plus work environment

The two aspects have traditionally been combined when workforce effectiveness metrics have been developed. However, they are unique aspects of the "input," as the table below shows:

Talent	Focuses on the talent bank of people available to the organization – in effect its "inventory of talent" available as an input to the business model. This is a qualification, capability, and availability type of measure.
Culture	Focuses on the environment that exists within which work is to take place (the crucible for talent). This is a willingness and readiness approach.

Progressive organizations spend considerable financial resources in areas such as pre-employment assessment, orientation of new employees, leadership development, team development, coaching and mentoring, which are all part of the investment to ensure the optimum working environment that supports collaboration, cooperation, communications, and collective commitment to organizational purpose.

Many organizations also invest in ways to better understand the unique personalities of individuals, so that teams and "group work" can be more effectively managed; such investment often extends to pre-employment assessments. This important area of building and sustaining human capital is further explored in a later chapter; however, the point here is that this is an "invisible" aspect of human capital reporting, and it carries risk.

Not only is leadership important in creating the optimum environment for the performance of human capital, leadership must also reflect a focus on "managing the system" and not retain a functional view alone (this functional bias remains one of the challenges in moving toward integrated reporting, as many metrics remain the responsibility of a functional head). As discussed earlier, human capital is at a point in its evolution where quality management was some 40 years ago, when quality was the responsibility of the quality department, until it was realized that quality was a systemic capability not limited to management as a function. Today's HR managers have limited capability to develop meaningful HR metrics and create the optimum climate for the optimization of human capital unless the "way we do things around here" is a common theme of inclusion and engagement, initiated at the very top of the organization and deployed as part of the strategic operational system everywhere.

For many years, the concept of "silo busting" was a focus for building high-performance organizations. (In my own experience of working with senior financial managers, making the move from a financial specialist / accountant into a management role, such as a Controller or CFO, I constantly placed emphasis on the importance to "think more like a general manager.") While the CEO can be thought of as "the integrator," the senior leadership team must also work together to manage the "system" that they are responsible for. When considering system performance, metrics must combine both functional and system thinking.

The following extract from the introductory chapter to my recent book on corporate culture[13], demonstrates the challenge faced by organizational leaders – at all levels – in creating and sustaining an environment (culture) that optimizes human performance:

---

[13] Shepherd, Nick, *Corporate Culture – combining values and purpose*, (2021), Eduvision Inc. / Jannas Publications, KDP / Amazon.

As human resources have become increasingly important to business performance, so has the challenge for leadership to create an environment where every dollar spent is an investment and not a cost. I remember being asked, some years ago by a major global pharmaceutical company, to attend one of their senior executive meetings and explain what this "thing" called corporate culture really is. Even asking the question was troubling.

There is no right culture. No consulting firm can tell you how to solve your corporate culture "issues." It is like going to a marriage counsellor and asking them to "fix" your marriage. No two relationships are the same because no two people are the same. It is the same in business. Culture is unique to each organization. What makes it REALLY hard is that people are unique, fickle, and different. Many of their actions are driven as emotional responses, no matter how "committed" they are.

But make no mistake; every organization has a culture – even if it has never been defined as such. This is a broad and inclusive area. It is about values and principles; about ethics and beliefs; about hiring approaches and pay principles; it is about communications, collaboration, and cooperation; it is about silos and territorial management; it is about trust, fairness, and transparency. It is also about the underlying approaches to suppliers and customers; to regulators; to investors and owners; to family members. It is about relationships with society and community. It is about how the work gets planned and executed. It is about how direction is given and problems are solved. Everything. That is why it is so hard.

This developing interest in corporate culture is the awakening of the realization that human capital must both led and managed. Human capital is flexible and capable of choosing between employers if the work environment is not satisfying. Consistency of approach by managers is a core aspect of building trust and demonstrating fairness – both foundations for an effective culture. The financial impact of a poor culture is not reflected in operating results but buried as part of ongoing costs. In the companion book to *Corporate Culture, The Cost of Poor Culture*[14] demonstrates the unseen impact of not ensuring an effective climate for optimizing human performance.

Several leading organizations have been able to clearly demonstrate this link between performance and employee engagement. These include Gallup (Q12 report on performance[15]), McKinsey Global Institute (2019 report on intangibles) and others.

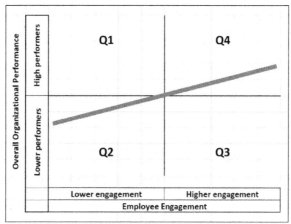

Figure 4-11 Correlation between engagement and performance

This is shown as chart 4.11 that suggests a strong correlation between employee engagement – a key driver of a positive culture, and overall system / organizational performance. The solid line shows a trend - typically lower performers exhibit lower levels of performance (Q2) while those with a higher engagement score (Q4) show higher performance. The message is clear; there is a link between engagement and performance of the the system or business model.

---

[14] Shepherd, Nick. *The Cost of Poor Culture*, 2021, Eduvision Inc. / Jannas Publications, KDP / Amazon.
[15] Gallup 2020 Q12 Report as of October 25, 2021. https://www.gallup.com/workplace/321725/gallup-q12-meta-analysis-report.aspx

4.5   The struggle for meaningful metrics

The struggle for the few critical metrics that really add value to both decision makers and external report users, can be illustrated by this old story:

> *A man was out walking his dog one day, when he was surprised by a hot air balloon crash landing close by. Dusting himself down, the balloonist walked over to the man with the dog and asked where he was.*
>
> *The man with the dog, thought for a moment and said, "You are about 2 feet off the ground in a wicker basket in the middle of a green field".*
>
> *The balloonist replied, "You're a CPA aren't you" The man said "Yes, how did you know?" The balloonist replied, "It was simple really, the information you gave me was precise, accurate and totally useless!"*

In Chapter 3, "The basic foundations," the various existing approaches were discussed, including the development and application of the ISO 30414 guideline. There is a growing frustration and concern about the proliferation of corporate reporting which is leading to significant amounts of narrative information being released, many different types of metrics being used, and a lack of audits, comparability, and consistency. In general, the business community is beginning to say, "We need standardization, and we need it now." This may be valid for some of the more mature areas of reporting, such as climate change (natural capital), but several other areas remain as works in progress. One of the leading proponents of a framework for a consistent approach is the World Economic Forum (WEF), which includes many CEOs of global organizations. The WEF made the following points in an article headed, *Here's why comparable ESG reporting is crucial for investors* [16]:

- Investors are increasingly challenging companies to take more action on climate change.
- At the moment, there is no comparable, transparent data to measure corporate resilience and progress on environmental, social, and governance (ESG) issues.
- By supporting the World Economic Forum's Stakeholder Capitalism Metrics, investors can help progress towards better ESG reporting worldwide.

The article then goes on to mainly discuss climate change, although it does point out that it is *"more than climate change"* and continues, *"Climate change is critical, but it is not the only environmental impact we need to measure. Sustainable value creation also depends on protecting fresh water, fertile land, and ecosystems. A business cannot succeed in a society that fails, and of the three ESG elements, 'social' now ranks equally high in importance for investors, according to the Edelman Trust Barometer. The SCM capture both social and environmental impacts."* The question is, Do the WEF metrics start to provide an integrated approach that provides visibility into the issue of integration?

The WEF proposal sets out four principal groupings – pillars – of Governance, Planet, People and Prosperity. (It is interesting to note that the framework is the original "triple bottom line" plus governance, proving the longevity of the original idea!) These four pillars are linked directly to the UN SDGs, then supported by 21 core principles and 34 expanded principles (see Table 4.4.).

These 55 WEF metrics draw heavily on the GRI guidelines; they also reflect other initiatives that WEF has been involved with, such as the Embankment

---

[16] https://www.weforum.org/agenda/2021/07/comparable-esg-investors/ July 8, 2021

Project for Inclusive Capitalism (EPIC), the Task Force on Climate Related Financial Disclosures (TCFD); the Capital Coalition (in particular the 2016 Natural Capital Coalition), and work related to global competitiveness reports and infrastructure development.

It also links with selected SASB disclosures and established approaches, such as the Carbon Disclosure Project (CDP), ISO 14008:2019 Monetary evaluation of environmental impacts and related environmental aspects, and several other reports, studies, and recommendations. Metrics in Table 4.4 are shown as core ("C") and enhanced ("E").

Table 4.4 World Economic Forum reporting topics

Pillar	UN SDG link	# Of "C"	# Of "E"	Comments
Governance	12, 16, 17	6	6	Links strongly to GRI and EPIC
Planet	6, 7, 12, 13, 14, 15	4	12	Links to Natural Capital Coalition, ISO 14008, and others
People	1, 3, 4, 5, 8, 10	6	9	Strong links to GRI and several others
Prosperity	1, 8, 9, 10	5	7	Several links and adaptations to GRI also FASB and others.
TOTAL		21	34	

Focusing on the people metrics (see Table 4.5), it can be seen that many are similar to the traditional frameworks, while some of the additions reflect social aspects of human capital outcomes; some of the latter are part of existing EU guidelines – in particular related to human rights (which is consistent with the SDGs).

Table 4.5 WEF People related metrics – core and expanded

People metric	Core	Expanded
Diversity and inclusion	1	
Pay equity %	2	
Wage level %	3	
Risk for incidents of child, force, or compulsory labour	4	
Health and safety %	5	
Training provided # and $	6	
Pay gap % $		1
Discrimination and harassment incidents (#) and total amount of monetary losses		2
Freedom of association and collective bargaining at risk %		3
Human rights review, grievance impact & modern slavery (# and %)		4
Living page %		5
Monetized impact of work related incidents on organization (#, $)		6
Employee well being (#, %)		7
Number of unfilled skilled positions (#, %)		8
Monetized impact of training - increased learning capacity as a result of training intervention ($, %)		9

More details on each of the proposed WEF metrics can be found in their 2020 report[17]. The good news is that several of the human capital metrics start to build the linkage with financial resources, as well as address the climate in terms of organizational culture.

17

http://www3.weforum.org/docs/WEF_IBC_Measuring_Stakeholder_Capitalism_Report_2020.pdf

Why is change needed? In summary, because this evolution to a new business model mirrors past "sea changes" to economic activity, which resulted in the system of corporate reporting and accountability that exists today – change is necessary!

What is needed is new thinking – a paradigm change that moves beyond trying to fit current and future reporting needs into a framework that was created for another era. **What exists today** for effective corporate governance results in surprises for managers, boards, and shareholders; it is also driving complexity and cost because there is a limited willingness to step back from today's reality and start with a "clean slate."

Corporate governance was addressed by the author in 2005[18], at a time when business was focused on managing technology and trying to account for intellectual capital. For several years, serious scandals had been impacting corporations and were being blamed on poor governance. There were headlines in the press, such as *"Directors asleep at the wheel."*

Thus, today, governance is a critical starting point for a new way of thinking about the six capitals, and specifically the role of human capital. Although the dates and eras are general and for illustrative purposes only, Figure 4.4 demonstrates how governance and corporate reporting –and financial reporting in particular – have changed.

---

[18] Shepherd, Nick, A., *Governance, Accountability and Sustainable Development*, 2005, Thomson, Canada.

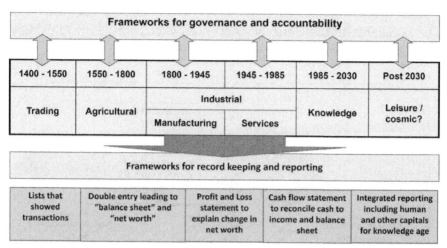

Figure 4-12 Evolution of governance as a driver of change

As can be seen from Figure 4.12, as business and social order have changed, so have the approaches to governance, including the way underlying records are maintained and activities and accountabilities are reported.

The foundation of business has long been one of "trading transactions," which were recorded as lists of who owed whom how much. As the economic era changed, so the type of governance approaches and structures also changed. When Pacioli developed double-entry bookkeeping, the lists of transactions became the basis of a balance sheet – still showing assets (what an individual owned), liabilities (what they owed to others), and the difference – their net worth. As economic activity became more complex (and faster), users wanted to know why their net worth had changed, so a statement that showed all the current trans-actions was developed; this is now the P&L or earnings statement. As accounting became more complex still, users started to ask how the change in their net worth didn't show up as more money in the bank, and so the cash flow statement was developed, bringing us to the current situation. Behind all of this, there has been an evolution of the various standards that ensure consistency of information being presented (readers will be familiar with the Generally Accepted Accounting Principles, GAAP). Figure 4.13 demonstrates that evolution.

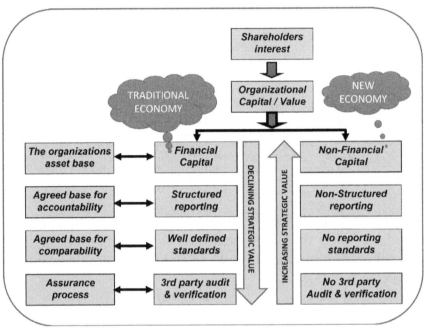

Figure 4-13 The evolution from financial to other "capitals"

It has already been established that shareholder interests are now stakeholder interests, as per the statement related to "Purpose" by the Business Round Table. This reflects the *declining* strategic importance of focusing on financial reporting, which is now well-established with rules and standards, and the *increasing* strategic importance of other areas of reporting. However, it takes time to develop new approaches – reflect on how long the underlying financial reporting framework has taken to develop and is *still* developing.

Management can learn a lot about the need for, and challenges to, change, by observing the evolution of scientific ideas. Modern science differs from all previous traditions of knowledge in three critical ways or stages:

1. The willingness to admit ignorance, in particular the willingness to accept that what we think we know may be wrong (no idea, concept, theory, or tradition is sacred or beyond challenge).
2. The centrality of observation and mathematics – the ability to connect observations and use mathematical tools to create comprehensive theories.
3. The acquisition of new powers – moving beyond theories to acquire new powers and, thence, develop new technologies.

It is interesting to note that, in finance, stage 2 already seems to be rapidly developing with the adoption of human analytics around management of the workforce. It is hoped this will lead to stage 3. However, stage 1 needs some work, and this is where different governance thinking resides. (Some years ago, in a book co-authored with Dr Peter Smyth, I specifically suggested that good leaders for the emerging economy would be those who were "reflective" in nature but were open to engagement and involvement![19]).

In Part 1, I hope that I have made the case for a paradigm shift, as well as outlining how we have "been here before," in terms of stepping back and re-thinking what needs to be done. In Part 2, the next chapter will explore what a "new" approach might look like. Be prepared to develop some "stage 1" thinking and be open-minded to how the reporting of human capital might proceed!

Why human capital metrics are needed – summary
• Existing human capital metrics are based on traditional HR thinking.

---

[19] Shepherd, Nick A., and Smyth, Peter J., *Reflective Leaders and High-Performance Organizations: How Effective Leaders Balance Task and Relationship to Build High Performing Organizations*, 2012, iUniverse.

- Society is looking more closely at the link between corporate activity and human impact.
- Global organizations such as the UN have issued guidelines for human capital centric societal development.
- Business is realizing that it must respond to all stakeholders and not focus purely on shareholders.
- For many organizations the highest consumption of cash resources is people compensation.
- In many organizations a large proportion of people are employed in building and sustaining intangible infrastructure.
- The importance of human capital is growing as economies shift to a knowledge / information base.
- Human capital is paid to create other intangible capitals – relationships, intellectual – that sustain business capability.
- The risks inherent in "human capital centered" organizations are often not clearly visible.
- The greater proportion of an investor's value is now represented by intangibles – not reported or audited as part of regular reporting.
- There is a strong link between human capital and organizational value creation, both economic and other.
- Many suggested frameworks for reporting have been developing that incorporate human capital.
- There is a strong link between the "health" / "quality" of the work environment and the performance of human capital, and hence the organization.
- Current metrics being used to populate these new frameworks have not evolved to a mature level.

Why human capital metrics are needed – checklist

- Is thinking about human capital metrics driven by traditional HR reports or future integrated reporting needs?

- Is the organization familiar with the evolving frameworks for integrated thinking and reporting?
- Is thinking about future human capital metrics aligned with and driven by people as a key strategic resource?
- Is human capital being approached as a strategic resource that creates and sustains economic value?
- Are outputs and outcomes from human capital as a creator of intangibles being identified, evaluated, measured, and monitored?
- Has organizational culture been recognized as a key enabler of human performance?
- Is the organization aware of and / or measuring its culture through metrics such as employee engagement?
- Does the organization know how much financial resource is being expended to create and sustain intangibles that are not reflected in financial records?
- Are key human metrics driven by activities, tasks, processes, and projects that, through human effort, convert key goals and objectives into desired outputs and outcomes?
- Are human capital metrics being used to measure desired results (goals) against actual results?
- Are human capital metrics the result of measuring strategically critical activities and outputs?

PART 2

Part 2 expands on more recent approaches to human capital reporting, in particular the focus on human capital within an integrated reporting context. A framework for reporting human capital aspects is described, followed by a discussion on what metrics can be developed and potentially used to populate the suggested framework. The final chapters discuss the importance and challenges of reporting organizational culture and the possible need for a whole-system metric to assess the overall health of a human-centric business.

5 Integrated human capital reporting

This part of the book builds the bridge between the current direction of HR metrics and the shift that needs to take place to link HR strategy to value creation and societal benefit. The goals of the next phase of human capital metrics must be to:

- Develop an effective framework for human capital metrics:
  - o complement and support existing and developing approaches to the corporate reporting of human capital, in particular integrated thinking; and
  - o present metrics in groups that align with core activities / initiatives / aspects of business thinking and human resources / people management.
- Incorporate metrics that provide value-adding information for enhanced risk management and decision making:
  - o include the rapidly developing area of "workplace environment" often termed as corporate culture or employee engagement;
  - o start to build better bridges between human capital and the implications on financial capital;
  - o include core areas of existing reporting on human capital related to the management of human resources; and
  - o ensure human capital outcomes enable clear linkage with organizational goals and objectives.

While many people and organizations are trying to develop new frameworks within which to report human capital, that train left the station many years ago. The present framework is Integrated Reporting or <IR> which was developed by the International Integrated Reporting Council (IIRC). In early 2021, the IIRC merged with the Sustainability Accounting Standards Board (SASB) to create the Value Reporting Foundation. The strategic goal of effective HR reporting must be to build a family of metrics that fit within the <IR> framework and populate the human capital requirements. Through this, HR reporting becomes part of an integrated whole.

While some may place human capital metrics into the category of "non-financial reporting," this makes little sense, as human capital – people – represents the single largest consumer of financial capital in most organizations. To not report on human capital as it relates to financial capital is a key part of the problem; moving thinking away from people purely as a cost and shifting the focus to people as a value creating investment is the way forward.

Financial reporting, and the development of effective human capital reporting are strategically and critically inter-dependent. People are also material to the well-being of an organization and its ability to sustain its value for owners and investors. This was demonstrated clearly in 2021 in the SEC investigation into Activision Blizzard on matters pertaining the materiality of disclosures around human capital. This was not new – there have been many investigations following financial problems and failures, such as Carillion in the UK, that revealed issues related to human capital – especially organizational culture – which started at the top.

Human capital is also the prime creator of other critical capitals employed in many organizations. Human capital creates relationships: it develops cooperation and collaboration; and it drives innovation and creativity. Investment of financial resources in human capital leads to the creation of intellectual capital, manufactured capital, social and relationship capital, as well as creating a mindset for the protection of natural capital.

5.1 Develop a reporting framework

The first sub-section discusses how human capital reporting should align with the thinking of the integrated reporting framework; for many, this will be familiar territory, as many business models incorporate the concepts of inputs, activities, outputs, and outcomes. Human capital metrics fit quite well into one of these four general categories. If one thinks about building a reporting matrix, these four areas would form the horizontal axis.

In the second section, we will develop a vertical axis for the model that is built around the concept of human capital. What is it that needs to be reported? How can these metrics be thought about, created, and grouped in similar categories? Many traditional HR metrics provide information on how well the HR functional processes (activities) are operating and this will form one core group of metrics that need to be reported, but there are other important aspects of human capital management that are not managed by human resources yet are critical to business success and impacted by actions and decisions outside the HR function.

5.1.1 Complement and support integrated thinking

At this point in the evolution of reporting, it is apparent where some of the key "stakes in the ground" have landed. The IIRC framework, which remains a key aspect of the Value Reporting Foundation, appears to be the de facto base, especially as it depicts the six capitals, including human capital, within the emerging business model.

This framework provides the conceptual basis within which human capital or people metrics need to be reported. It establishes the purpose for integrated reporting within which HR metrics fit. It sets out a "thinking process" for determining the scope of such metrics, and addresses aspects such as identifying stakeholders and determining materiality. Importantly, this model has already been adopted for annual reporting by many leading global organizations and is also supported by many regulators, investors, investment advisors and financial organizations.

The scope of human metrics should be linked back to the IIRC statement of how an organization "*...creates, preserves or erodes value over time.*" Part 1 of the International Framework document from IIRC lays out all the underlying principles (Figure 5.1). Human capital is one of six core capitals or resources utilized in a business model. Integration of these capitals is "what management does" to create value.

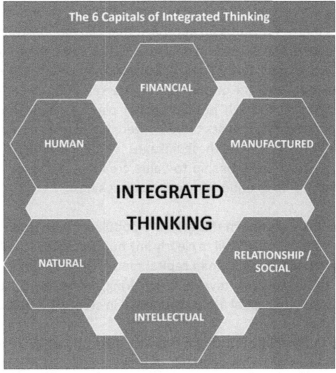

Figure 5-1 The six capitals of integrated thinking (IIRC)

In 2016, the IIRC also issued a publication, *Creating Value – The value of human capital reporting*[20], which can help in understanding the changing concept of value and the underlying value chain / value creation thinking.

As can be seen from Figure 5.1, the six capitals of the <IR> approach are intended to be seen as the combined resources that an organization employs within its business model, through which "value" is created. This integrated approach has become the basis of Environmental, Social and Governance (ESG) reporting. However, while current approaches are well-developed in the area of environment, in particular climate change, the reporting of other areas such as human capital, is under-developed.

Populating a reporting framework will require us to move beyond the traditional metrics towards an approach that can demonstrate the critical role that people play in contributing to creating value for an organization. Value, in "integrated" terms goes well beyond accounting value and should start to explain how an organization's market value is supported by a business system in which human capital plays a pivotal role. This will require some existing metrics to be utilized but also needs a new series to be sought out that creates these linkages. Additionally, metrics should go beyond reflecting "relationship to value creation" and look to achieve a causal relationship to underlying enterprise value.

Currently, many reports in this area are populated with traditional human resources metrics, which fail to clearly link human capital to value creation. This link is what mature human capital metrics must develop; it is *critical*, because the resources invested in hiring, developing, leading, and supporting human capital are instrumental in creating other capitals.

While the integrated reporting model identifies six unique capitals, there are strong inter-relations between most of these (see Figure 5.2). As an

---

[20] https://www.integratedreporting.org/resource/creating-value-board/

example, that will be discussed in more detail later, financial capital and human capital are totally inter-dependent. This inter-relationship is important when considering that human capital is a key resource that creates three of the other capitals. No longer do people just create products and services during activities within the conversion process from inputs to outputs - they now create "intangible capital."

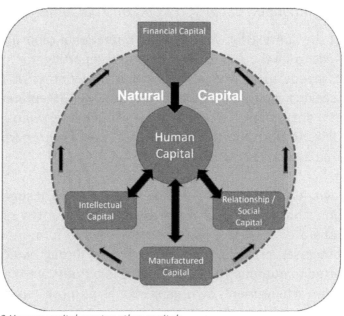

Figure 5-2 Human capital creates other capitals

Figure 5.2 demonstrates the role that human capital plays in the conversion process that creates other capitals. This reflects a core, underlying business change - especially the application of financial capital.

Historically, organizations spent a large amount of financial capital investing in tangible assets: e.g., plant, property, equipment, and inventory through which they created value – all tangible "stuff." The financial balance sheet showed that these assets still existed and still had value (verified by financial audits). In the last 30 years, however, instead of investing in tangible assets, organizations have been diverting cash to create and sustain "intangibles" – many of which are included in the other "capitals" identified in the IIRC model. The problem that this has created is that financial reporting and audits provide no information on the use of cash to create most intangible assets – they just kind of disappear. Effective human capital reporting becomes critical to be able to address this gap in information.

5.1.2   Applying input, activity, output, and outcome

Given that the context for strategic and operational reporting of human capital needs to fill the gap within integrated reporting, the presentation of metrics needs to be thought of within the context of that model. Readers seeking more background on the IIRC integrated reporting framework, are referred to the Value Foundation website[21], which provides links to both the thinking behind integrated reporting and the detailed framework and business model.

The framework is quite simple. As shown in Figure 5.3, it suggests that an organization's business model requires some or all of the six capitals in order to operate. These are its "resources," which form inputs that are used for processes, projects, activities, and tasks, through which the inputs are converted to outputs. The results of these outputs are then outcomes that are the achievement of organizational purpose, spanning *all* six capitals.

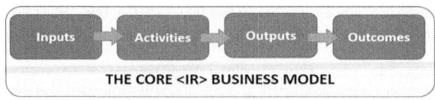

Figure 5-3 Achieving outcomes / purpose by converting inputs to outputs

How would these four steps apply to human capital? In simple terms, workforce availability underlies the input, in terms of both people who are

---

[21] https://www.valuereportingfoundation.org/

available and the tacit qualifications that they bring with them. These are then "employed" in the operational processes of "getting the work done." This is the process of conversion input to outputs resulting in the products and services that an organization creates which then achieves its purpose – the outcome. Traditionally the model may have looked like that presented in Figure 5.4

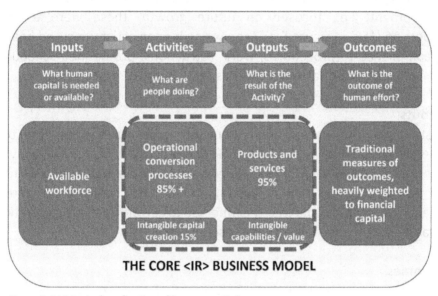

Figure 5-4 Historical application of human capital

Input

Historically, the "available workforce" was the employees on the payroll plus a few part-time and temporary people. As a result of strategies such as supplier and customer partnering, the available workforce now includes many people outside the organization. Organizations have also adopted "rings of protection" so that the permanent workforce has often shrunk to be supplemented by contract, part-time and temporary people. "Just in time" (JIT) approaches now require the close coordination of workforce planning across the whole supply chain to achieve organizational goals and objectives. These represent big changes in the content of human capital input.

Activities
Traditionally, most employees were involved and engaged in activities that created products or delivered services (about 85%; see Figure 5.4). While some people were involved in areas such as sales or research and development, i.e., focused on future growth, these were a small proportion (15% in Figure 5.4). Monitoring human activity focused heavily on compliance to procedures, work instructions, pre-defined schedules, and other "directed" activity. This has now changed.

Outputs
Most of the outputs of labor were the products and services that generated revenues – possibly 95% of the output of human activity. Monitoring revenues to labor costs was a reasonable way of determining the effectiveness of human capital. While there were some people engaged in activities not directly connected to current revenue generation, it was a small proportion. This has also changed.

Outcomes
Outcomes are related to the achievement of organizational goals and objectives, and the work that people do is entirely focused on achieving these. Given the traditional input, activity, and output content indicated in Figure 5.4, outcomes were traditionally weighted towards the achievement of financial goals and objectives. Profitability would be high on the list while metrics such as Return on Investment (ROI) and Return on Invested Capital (ROIC) would also be used. Outcomes still need to be linked to the purpose, goals, and objectives of the organization – but these have changed from being heavily weighted to financial outcomes and typically now include intangibles and the other capitals.

The reality of what goes on inside the business model has changed so that many traditional HR metrics are inadequate or potentially misleading. It is important to note that in knowledge-based businesses a large proportion of people's effort is in the creation of intangibles; as discussed earlier, people are critical to the creation of relationship capital but also to the development of "system capability" that can deliver innovation, creativity, knowledge sharing, teamwork, effective communications, effective leadership, agility, and many other capabilities. People are also the creators – and often owners – of intellectual capital, especially when not codified. There is almost no visibility of these operational activities, nor do traditional HR metrics effectively assess productivity in these aspects. The more current approach to the input, activity, output, and outcome model might look like Figure 5.5.

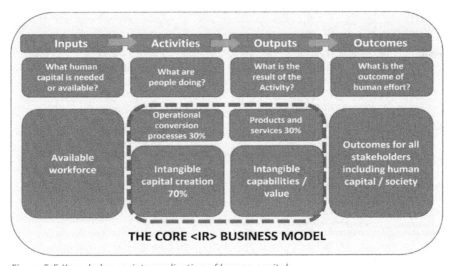

Figure 5-5 Knowledge society application of human capital

The key important change is that human effort applied to converting inputs to outputs is now much more heavily weighted to the creation of intangibles (say, 70%); Additionally, societal pressure is requiring that outcomes now be thought about not just in financial terms for the investor, but in human terms for society. Outcomes should also reflect value creation in terms of other capitals. Human capital is certainly contributing to financial outcomes through "value adding" to products and services but people are also creating system capabilities which form the foundation of organizational capability and continuity.

The challenge is that financial information currently ignores the amount of resources being used to fund human capital effort in these areas, and traditional HR metrics aggregate all costs related to human capital as the cost of creating current products and services. What will human capital reporting need to reflect within the new model? Table 5.1 lists the additional content in each of the four categories.

Table 5.1 Expanding content of input, activity, output, and outcome

STEP	TRADITIONAL CONTENT	ADDITIONAL CONTENT
Input	The total aggregate "pool" of human capital available as a resource input – both in terms of numbers and in qualifications, availability and skills, knowledge and capabilities.	The quality of the workforce in terms of engagement, commitment, leadership strength and aspect of culture. Also societal driven expectations such as diversity and inclusion.
Activity	Insight into the total application of human capital to the process of converting inputs to product and service outputs (that are sold to clients).	Insight into human activities through which human input is converted into intangible infrastructure and business system capabilities.
Output	The outputs of the processes and activities in terms of the creation of products, services and other activities.	Outputs related to activities necessary to create and sustain intangibles such as relationships, intellectual capitals.
Outcome	Measurement of outcomes against expectations (actual results vs. goals and objectives).	Expansion of business outcomes to include human activity relative to strategic areas like brand quality, recognition, knowledge base and others.

This change in each of the four categories will expand the breadth of human capital reporting required to populate and explain human capital performance within an integrated business model. Some existing metrics will work but additional metrics will be needed. Care will also be required in aggregation at too high a level to avoid operational performance being mixed with long-term capital creation performance.

As noted, traditional productivity measures might start to become misleading. Although metrics like HC-ROI do indicate more effective organizations, this is possibly because, as Jim Collins stated, "...*successful companies do thousands of things right every day.*" The basic IIRC model of "input – activity – output – outcome" can be seen as the horizontal axis for reporting human capital metrics. Existing metrics can be reviewed and used to populate one or more of these categories according to the best fit (see Figure 5.6). Are we assessing the stock of human capital resources available? If so, this would be our input. Are we looking at the performance of human capital? Then this would populate the activity area – and so on.

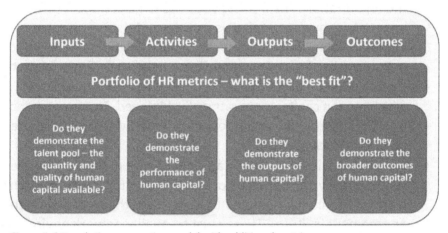

Figure 5-6 Populating a reporting model with additional metrics

This depiction may be overly simplistic and might lead to past approaches being applied where a new framework and approach fails to lead to new thinking. This can be solved by asking what types of metrics are needed to tell the story of human capital. This is where it becomes important both to step back and reflect on the organizational goals and objectives and to ask "what are people actually doing?". Clearly, much of the maturing of human capital metrics will only come about when the introduction of "integrated thinking" enables goals and objectives to be established that directly relate to the workforce and the importance of intangibles within the business model.

5.1.3   Developing metrics in meaningful "groups"

Reflecting on discussions to date, five major aspects or categories of HR metrics emerge that should be considered to build a portfolio. These evolve from the thinking that:

- Present financial reporting, driven by standards, is unable to consider many of the investments made in people as an "asset" to the organization. The link between the large cash flow consumed / invested in human capital is poorly understood yet has major strategic value and operational impact relative to the effective management of human capital. There need to be **financial metrics**.
- Organizational success is highly driven by the effectiveness with which human capital is operationally deployed. This is not managed by HR but forms part of the "organizational system." There need to be **operational metrics**.
- The effectiveness of human capital deployment has been proven to reflect heavily on the quality of leadership and the way in which the work environment operates ("How we do things around here" – engagement, culture). There must be quality or **work environment / culture / engagement metrics**)
- Increasing societal pressures are impacting corporate reputations, brands and "license to operate," and key aspects of human capital policies and management, as a core aspect of corporate governance, have a major impact. There must be good **governance metrics**.
- The effectiveness of the human resources function and the processes and activities it performs are a core factor in overall organizational effectiveness related to human capital. There must be **HR process metrics**.

Using these five major groupings, a framework can be developed, within which all human capital metrics should be able to fit (see Table 5.2). The absence of metrics within any category might suggest an area for development.

Table 5.2 The five types of human capital metrics

ASPECT	CONTENT
Financial	Bridge building: financially related aspects of human capital investment such as "sunk costs" related to acquisition, orientation, leadership development, together with activity costs related to spending on intangibles not shown by accounting.
Operational	Deployment: effectiveness / productivity from people deployed in processes, activities, tasks and projects related aspects of human capital – embracing ALL deployments not just products and services.
Leadership	Culture / work environment: aspects of work environment addressing employee engagement, leadership quality, collaboration effectiveness, and all aspects relative to "the health of the workplace."
Governance / Social	Governance: metrics related to addressing societal needs including mandatory statutory reporting and also policies / decisions driven by brand, reputation and to be seen as a "good corporate citizen."
HR Management	HR effectiveness: all HR processes and activities that are managed and activated as the underpinning foundation for day-to-day HR management (recruitment, training and development) that support BOTH operational effectiveness AND employee engagement / satisfaction.

Because human capital has such a major impact on financial resources, key aspects that cannot be reported using standard accounting principles (GAAP) can be developed as supplemental metrics that start to build a bridge between financial capital and human capital. This is the first category.

The second is the operational category; this addresses metrics that relate to the availability, use, outputs, and outcomes of human capital or talent in an operational context; many of these metrics may already exist and tend to reflect what "inventory" of people is available and how effectively they operate in doing their assigned tasks and activities. Many metrics will be missing operationally because, in traditional reporting, it was assumed that all human capital performance was related to current outputs and outcomes and did not include work on building intangible capital. In the growing importance of value creation in non-financial terms, this becomes an important aspect.

The third category of metrics is the potentially developing or new aspect that extracts the leadership areas that are traditionally buried within operational performance. Leadership is about empowerment and engagement of the workforce and is a strong risk indicator related to both sustainability and resilience of the enterprise. This category would be the "home" for leadership, culture, engagement, and the health and performance of other work "climate or environment."

The next category of metrics demonstrate the organization's areas of social responsibility both to statutory requirements and to acting as a good corporate citizen; this is key to sustainability of value in areas such as brand and reputation. When governance (in ESG) is discussed, it would be metrics in this area that start to link together human capital and the "license to operate" related to the public's perception of how the organization behaves. This would probably embrace areas such as ethical conduct. Ethics remains a very challenging area for business; unethical conduct has a negative impact on corporate reputation and public perception, but it is not illegal. Thus, organizations that choose to take discretionary action to protect their reputation might have critical key metrics in this category. (The issues around "tax planning" to minimize corporate taxes might be a key area of focus.)

The final category provides metrics that demonstrate performance of the underlying HR processes. Effective management of human capital depends upon a foundation of good HR management; these metrics would probably be some of the more common and might be faster to use for benchmarking and comparability.

Putting together the five types or categories discussed and the four business model stages of input, activity, output and outcomes, the overall reporting matrix will look like something like Figure 5.7.

Aspects of resource / capital management	Input	Activity	Output	Outcome
1. Financial investment in human resources. Goal - understand cash flow investment in people (managing the "asset" that is invested in)				
2A. Operational management of human resources Goal - effective management (use) of human resources				
2B. Leadership of human resources Goal - sustaining optimum climate for human resources				
3 "Good Governance" Goal compliance, social responsibility, and optimum talent pool				
4. HR management Goal - effective operation of HR processes				

Figure 5.7 Example of a human capital reporting matrix

Within each of the five categories, a goal has been added to further develop the purpose for each grouping. As in many decisions, the names, titles, approaches, and other suggestions may not be perfect, and others may have ideas around modification. That is fine – as indicated much earlier, this is time of evolution and experimentation.

The next stage will be to start populating this framework with human capital metrics that provide insights into the performance, value creation, risk, and accountability of the human element of organizational activity and resources. This will start with an assessment of what is needed.

5.2 Populating the framework

The purpose of having human capital metrics is to help decision making and to identify risk, both internally and externally. The metrics need to be thought about as a hierarchy, so that at the Board level, the "critical few" provide adequate information to ensure compliance, risk management and oversight; at the "C" suite level, the critical few should not only provide adequate information for decision making, but it should be structured in such a way that problems can be identified and traced to the root cause, for action to be taken. At lower levels, metrics will be developed to help manage specific areas of operational accountability.

While the temptation might be to just start placing existing metrics somewhere in the framework, there are a few areas from the last section to be considered first that are important for developing a foundation for any kind of metrics development. Metrics form an essential part of organizational strategy and, as such, must have some linkage – either compliance with statutory regulations or other mandatory policies, or be linked directly to the purpose goals and objectives of the organization. Whatever people are doing, they are doing it for a purpose. Measuring what is happening is only of value if we also know what *should* be happening.

5.2.1 Human capital as a part of the "system"

Integrated thinking is about looking at organizational activity from a different perspective. The business model of inputs, activities, and outputs reflects the "system" that has been created (the business model); the intent of this model is to convert organizational purpose, along with goals and objectives (and underpinned by behavioural values), into the desired results or outcomes (see Figure 5.8). A key aspect of ESG thinking, along with the broadening of the category of stakeholders impacted by the system's activities, is to recognize that the day-to-day activities that take place within the system have a much greater impact than just delivering profits to shareholders.

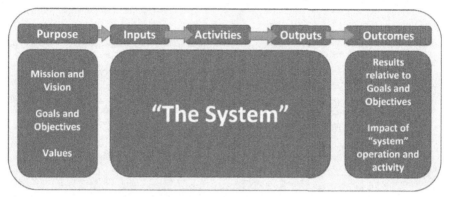

Figure 5.8 Ideas, execution, and outcomes

While models such as <IR> focus on inputs, activities, outputs, and outcomes, the reality is that the business model is put in place to achieve a *purpose*. The goals and objectives that stem from this purpose are ultimately the things that outcome metrics need to report. The high-level questions must be: Is the system we put in place working, how well is it working, and is it producing the outcomes that were desired?

To develop an effective set of metrics for human capital (and all others), this model must be the foundation, subject to one, key, golden rule.

> ***OUTCOMES are created by the combined (integrated) operation of the system; outcome measures are therefore principally driven by comparison between desired outcomes (goals and objectives) and actual outcomes.***

This means that there will be outcome metrics for human capital – but that these will probably reflect the human impact from the operation of the system. Note that in Figure 5.9, the "workforce" is shown as an input, but that input takes place within a work environment – so effective metrics would assess *both* the workforce *and* the work environment (possibly as culture or engagement or some other system-level metric).

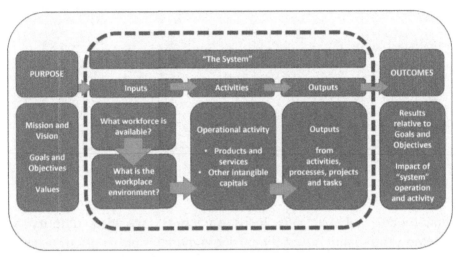

Figure 5-9 Human capital within "the system" concept

While it is hard to assess the financial "value" of human output (as it is integrated within other aspects), it is not hard to measure things like health, well-being and societal impact.

This focus on the "system" is important in developing all metrics, in that value creation comes as a result of the system's integration and conversion activity, rather than from any one of the input capitals. Each is important as an element of the formula needed to achieve organizational purpose. However, value creation in its broad sense comes from the effective combination of *all* resources. This has always been true of financial capital and is equally true of all other capitals.

5.2.2   Starting at the end with OUTCOMES

This may seem a strange step but, unless the desired outcomes are clear, any reporting will fall short of adding value to the stakeholders it is designed for. The organization is a system put in place to achieve certain pre-defined expectations; there is a danger that, without understanding these goals and objectives, and the activities designed to achieve them, improvement efforts will rest on exhortations to "try harder". This will never work. (Interestingly, this was a foundational aspect of the work done in quality management some 50 years or so ago.)

The development of any system of metrics is to ensure that performance is moving towards planned results. The Plan–Do–Check–Act (PDCA) model (Figure 5.10) was developed by the American statistician and physicist, Walter Shewhart – considered the father of PDCA. There is a story of W. Edwards Deming, American engineer and statistician, who is often seen as the father of quality management and in particular Statistical Process Control (SPC), who believed strongly that quality management and improvement must be built into the overall process of management. The PDCA model became well-known as a core part of Deming's approach, and is even referred to as the Deming Cycle.

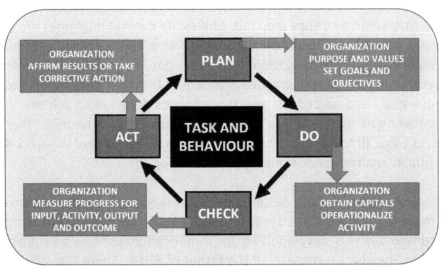

Figure 5-10 The PDCA model at enterprise level

The PDCA model is a perpetual system of metrics, whose development "populates" the CHECK aspect.

1. PLAN (what you want to do): In this illustration, that encompasses both the outcomes in terms of products and services and the desired behaviours – the "culture" part of strategy – and includes planning for the resources needed to convert plans into action.
2. DO: Establish systems and processes, task, activities, projects, and all the "structures" needed to convert inputs into outputs based on the desired plan. This includes accessing all the resources that are needed for the conversion process.
3. CHECK: Develop approaches (*metrics*) that check progress against the plans, and that can be evaluated on a continuing basis. This will include both "activity" type metrics and outputs and outcomes.
4. ACT: Based on the metrics, make changes and adjustments to bring actual results back into line with plans. This step also feeds back into planning, so that plans can also be updated and amended to reflect changing goals and objectives in the future.

Note that the model in Figure 5.10 shows the whole *organization* view. An exact replica would apply to each of the six capitals to form the planning, execution, checking, and act elements of the whole business model.

Human capital is an intrinsic part of the resources needed to make the business model work; thus, human capital metrics must be developed to support every step of the model; to assess plans, support and monitor execution, and assess actual results against plans.

This is the reason for starting with OUTCOMES – if there are no clear goals established with measurable objectives, it will be impossible to build an effective framework for human capital reporting.

What types of business goals link directly to human capital outcomes?

In a human-centric world, the answer must go beyond statements like, "We believe in people as our greatest asset." It should start with a high-level statement such as, "We propose to create a harm-free environment where we can attract and retain the right people at the right time, to ensure our organizational growth and success." This might then be translated into goals and objectives, such as to:

- sustain our position as employer of choice within the top quartile in our industry;
- sustain our position in the top quartile of employee engagement in our industry sector;
- achieve zero unfilled strategically critical positions at any time;
- ensure all strategically identified positions have a succession plan ready in a maximum of 2 years;
- sustain an unplanned turnover rate in the best / lowest quartile in our industry;
- achieve zero unplanned non-compliances or unethical behaviours; and

- sustain a harm free work environment in both physical and mental health.

These are the kind of expectations against which outcomes can be measured. Additionally, the whole structure and management of human resources at both strategic and operational levels will be designed to deliver the desired outcomes. As an example, HR process metrics would be established to ensure HR processes are functioning in a way that underpins and supports the desired outcomes. This is what will then start to populate the HR metrics in the outcome aspect.

5.2.3   Metrics – from plan to action

Effective HR planning should ensure that all resources are applied in a manner that supports the desired HR objectives as well as supporting and aligning with the needs of other operational areas. This is a core challenge – to shift human resources management away from a focus on HR infrastructure and processes towards a whole-system approach.

While HR management is responsible for the processes through which the necessary talent is acquired, much of the management of human capital rests with people outside the HR function. This requires that human capital plans and objectives are developed that focus on the desired outcomes. An effective human-centric planning approach will look at *all* aspects of the business model that impact human performance. This strategic planning approach to human capital will focus on both the operational management of people and the environment that is created within which they are to operate. HR cannot control these aspects of people management, so that policies, structures, procedures, and all other elements of the business model that impact people must also be addressed, monitored, measured, and reported on.

This is a key area in which effective approaches to human capital management have been developing, and many of them are starting to be embedded in leading practices as well as within international (ISO) standards on human capital management, as listed in Table 5.3.

Table 5.3 Some of the major ISO documents related to people

ISO Number	Title
ISO 10667- 1:2020	Procedures and methods to assess people in work and organizational settings – Part 1 Requirements for clients
ISO 10667- 2:2020	Procedures and methods to assess people in work and organizational settings – Part 2 Requirements for service providers
ISO 10018:2020	Guidelines for engaging people (part of quality management)
ISO 30401:2018	Knowledge Management Systems – Requirements
ISO 30405:2016	HRM – Guidelines on Recruitment
ISO 30408:2016	HRM – Guidelines on human governance
ISO 30409:2016	HRM – Workforce planning
ISO 30415:2021	HRM – Diversity and inclusion

In addition to this list and the guidelines on the development of metrics already discussed, there are several other areas being developed, such as guidelines on learning and development, employee engagement, and workforce allocation. These are supported by workforce data quality that looks at the structures beneath the metrics to ensure effective data collection and validation.

Of course, these are also supported by many current courses and thinking around "whole-system" HRM that form part of university and college courses, professional designation qualifications, and leading practice documents issued by human resource management associations world-wide.

5.2.4 What to report – scope and materiality

Carrying out the initial "scope assessment" of human capital reporting has become more complex; the people that become part of an organization's human capital reporting are no longer the employees on the payroll. Since the era of downsizing, outsourcing, remote working, globalization, supply chain evolution and decentralization people are "everywhere."

Stakeholders for human capital can include employees, agencies, independents, retirees, suppliers, customers, regulators, auditors, politicians, trade association members – even the general public. The somewhat simplistic approach of focusing on employees can miss the strategic impact of people on other capitals; for example, if a service engineer, working for a sub-contractor who is contracted to support your products in the field, behaves poorly toward a client, this will affect *your* reputation. The client cares little about whose name is on that person's paycheck.

Materiality also needs to be considered broadly; many organizations consider their employees as a holistic group when determining materiality. This is probably true at two levels:

- without people there is no one to run the business; and
- the financial capital paid to people is one of the greatest material expenses.

However, when thinking on an "integrated" basis, materiality might be quite different. Firstly, not all employees are critical and hard to replace, so developing metrics based on a homogeneous group is probably invalid. One might say "some people are more material than others." (This is where the challenge of equality and fairness can become a discussion point.) An example might be the reality that a small group of design engineers are much more critical to the current operations and the future of the organization than people working in other areas. Materiality in this case has a different context.

Secondly, materiality of human capital reporting must also be considered on the broader base of how it may impact other capitals. In this case, the people employed by, for example, suppliers, customers, shipping agencies, employment agencies, or regulators might have a significant impact on an organization's capitals and yet not be included as a "material" item to be reported on.

A story comes to mind that illustrates this point, related to interactions with the customer. Jan Carlson, CEO of Scandinavian Airlines (SAS – many years ago), developed the phrase "moments of truth" when referring to interactions between employees and customers. Every time a "one-on-one" encounter took place, wherever it was, whoever was involved, it was a moment of truth that impacted the image / reputation of the company. So, a baggage handler was equally important to any other person in the organization in terms of impacting the company's brand and reputation. (In those days, baggage handlers usually worked for the airline – now they are probably outsourced or sub-contracted – usually driven by the lowest cost.)

Are such people material to your organization's social and relationship capital? Are they even involved in your HR "field of vision?"

Human capital and the reporting of its importance to strategy can go far beyond what is often thought about as materiality. In a multi-capital, integrated enterprise, monitoring of human capital will need to extend beyond traditional boundaries.

The following list includes the major drivers for reporting (though obviously some will require change). In summary, the goal of human capital metrics is to:

- report on all legislated or other mandatory compliance requirements related to human capital;
- report on all aspects of human capital that are considered critical for a continuing societal "license to operate;"
- identify and report on the linkage between human capital and all other capital outcomes that enhance organizational value;
- report and explain the financial implications of building, compensating, and sustaining the workforce as a critical organizational capital;
- assess and report on the operational effectiveness of the workforce on key organizational outcomes;
- assess and report the level of employee engagement as a key driver of sustainable performance; and
- assess and report on the performance of key infrastructure that supports the management of human capital.

5.2.5   *Workplace environment: Culture, and engagement*

The pool of people that an organization has access to forms the basis of the talent, experience, skills, competencies, and capabilities required to perform the work – the foundation of human capital as a core resource. This will remain a critical aspect of INPUT reporting. Theoretically, the next step will be ACTIVITY reporting, which will demonstrate the effectiveness and productivity of the workforce. In very simple terms, the more output that can be generated from a given level of input, the more productively a resource is being used. What is being aggregated within this simple productivity measure?

- The match between people's skills and workplace needs.
- The alignment between people's understanding of the company purpose, goals, and objectives, and the expectations of their own work.
- The effectiveness of the underlying work scheduling and planning processes.

- The effectiveness of underlying support processes in ensuring people have the right materials, tools, equipment, and support systems.
- The effectiveness of management, including leadership in motivating and supporting employees.
- The levels of collaboration, cooperation, and communication among and between individuals and other work areas.
- The impact on people of safe and healthy work practices as well as stress from absenteeism and workload.

In the last 20 years, it has been clearly proven that there is a correlation between activity performance and productivity, and what is referred to as employee engagement. Therefore, productivity metrics must be de-aggregated. The factors which contribute to engagement have become critically important in understanding the effectiveness of human capital and in seeking the root causes of opportunities for improvement.

This is a unique aspect of human capital performance that has emerged as the efforts of people have been re-directed towards continuous improvement, innovation, and creativity. It is critical in a knowledge economy and was well captured in the books about the Google culture[22] and about Amazon, Facebook, Apple, and Google[23], as well as in the various reports created by organizations such as Gallup, especially the Q12 reports.

An organization can have a well-qualified workforce but, if it is operating in a low-trust, low-commitment environment, its performance will be sub-optimum. This reduces its competitive advantage and, hence, its value. Assessing this "environmental" aspect will be an important area of human capital reporting. Reporting on the levels of knowledge, skills, compe-

---

[22] Schmidt, Eric, and Rosenberg, Jonathan, *How Google Works*, 2015, Grand Central.
[23] Galloway, Scott, *The Four*, 2017, Scott Galloway, Penguin Portfolio.

tencies, and capabilities is important but understanding the climate within which these attributes are being utilized is equally important.

This aspect of organizational performance is often referred to as "culture;" in other words, "the way we do things around here." Culture is a context for organizational activity; it can be referred to as the crucible within which the "activity" takes place. Creating a positive culture is part of investing in human capital; and sustaining a positive culture contributes towards sustaining value and reducing risk.

There is little insight provided to this aspect of organizational risk and sustainability, yet the impact is significant. As an example, in a 2109 Gallup survey, it was reported that organizations with a higher employee engagement score delivered 21% higher productivity and 22% higher profitability. Understanding the climate must be a key performance metric.

The graphic in Figure 5.11 illustrates the concept; while the model remains the same, both the effectiveness of the activities and the outputs being created are subject to two factors – the workforce itself and the work environment that exists within which they operate. The culture impacts human performance and, because of this, has an impact on the "value" of the workforce itself as well as on the operational performance in terms of outputs.

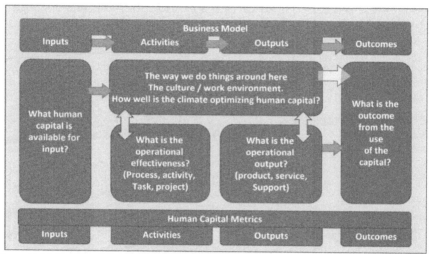

Figure 5-11 The "filter" for human capital

The resource pool for human capital is shown as the input, but as it is utilized in processes, projects, activities, and tasks, it may be considered to pass through a "filter" (Figure 5.11) that determines its overall effectiveness. Optimum performance comes from creating a climate that allows people to perform at their highest level; or, as Peter Drucker was quoted as saying, *"culture eats strategy for breakfast."* Therefore, metrics around human capital cannot be aggregated at the operational level if they are to provide any level of insight into risk and opportunity – they must include *both* the work climate *and* the operational activities and outputs.

Another way of thinking about the importance of culture is to reflect on the underlying assumption that organizations create value through their business model. Traditionally, this value is expressed in terms of financial performance; but, as society shifts its expectations of corporate accountability – often called its "license to operate" – value is expressed in a broader perspective. "Talent" – the knowledge, skills, experiences, competencies, and capabilities of people – provides the *potential* for value creation and performance, while culture is an enabler of performance; by "energizing" human talent and value creation, that will have an impact on outputs and outcomes. Figure 5.12 provides a representation of how this might look.

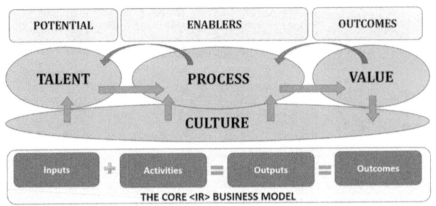

Figure 5-12 How culture enables people and process to create value

Culture exists as an underlying aspect of input, and it also underpins the operational process aspects of activities and outputs, as well as being an outcome of how the activity and process took place. The three aspects are also "iterative" in that an effective outcome in terms of a positive culture becomes an enhanced input for the next cycle. A positive reputation for work environment helps create a "draw" for the best talent, in effect creating a virtuous cycle. (Depletion of value occurs when the activities have a negative impact on culture, which is in effect a depletion of part of the human capital.)

Any approach to developing HR metrics must not only address the performance of human capital as a key aspect of the organization ability to execute its work of creating products and services, but also provide information about the management of the support functions which include the HR function itself.

The effectiveness of HR policies, processes, and support activities has an impact on overall company culture, so these must also be "measured to be managed." Like any other processes, they can be assessed in terms of cost, quality, time, and quantity; even tools like the Statistical Process Control (SPC) can be applied to ensure that processes operate "in control."

5.2.6 Building bridges – human and financial capital

While the scope of human capital includes people outside the organization, this discussion will focus on those paid directly by the company (either as employees, contractors, or other third parties). A large portion of cash flow is directed to compensating people, as shown in Figure 5.13.

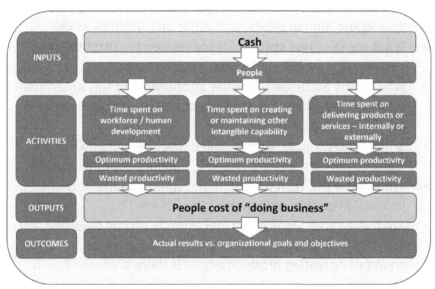

Figure 5-13 The need to understand where the money we pay people goes

This cash then goes to pay people to "do stuff." What they do, as has been discussed, is to spend time developing themselves as part of workforce "capability" building – this is referred to as part of the "value" of human capital. They are also paid to build other sorts of intangible infrastructure, such as supply chains and supplier relationships, intellectual capital and knowledge, customer or client relationships, as well as other important relationships with shareholders, fund managers, regulators, and many others. This creates the value attributed to other "capitals." Finally, some also spend time directly involved in creating current products and services. However, financially, *all* this cash (with a few allowed accounting exceptions) is charged as current expenses against income. This is the people cost of doing business. But clearly, assessing productivity by comparing total cash paid to people with revenues earned is not an accurate reflection of performance.

Looking at existing HR approaches to metrics and existing accounting, the following are unknown:

- How much of the current "people expense" is being invested in developing human capital and other intangible capitals?
- What are the "real costs" of labor related to current revenue creation that reflect underlying profitability?
- What is the accumulated value attributable to this investment (that will be reflected in the economic / market value of the business and thus its shares)?
- Is this "investment," that should deliver benefits (ROI) over multiple periods, being sustained, maintained, or depleted?
- What is the risk related to human capital and the potential financial impact of unplanned losses of staff?
- Are these three types of activity (human capital development, other intangible capital development, and product and service creation) operating productively or is there a waste of cash occurring?
- Do existing financial metrics tell the full cost impact of "loss of labor" such as turnover, absenteeism, short- or long-term disability.
- Is there any reporting that provides insight into any financial waste or loss that maybe occurring due to the quality or health of the "people–work environment?"

The question can also be asked related to the cash invested in building other intangibles that create "value" – both economic / financial and other

– to the organization: How much is the loss of a key supplier in terms of the financial costs of building the relationships and the inter-dependency of the infrastructure? While this is out of scope of human capital metrics, it demonstrates the importance of understanding what people are spending their time doing, and what strategic financial impact is occurring when these "capitals" are depleted or lost.

To understand the challenge of integration is to realize that the additional five capitals are not "add-on" components that are intended to drive more areas of silo-based functional reporting; they are the crystallization of management activities that have been occurring over many years, by diverting and investing financial resources into the creation of intangibles, most of which have remained invisible to investors. Not only has this created a growing gap between traditional accounting and market value, it has also created "new" capitals that form part of an integrated system *in combination with* financial capital.

Issues such as staff turnover now become a significant cost; not only is the cumulative investment in the person lost, but also the loss of tacit knowledge and experience has a broader impact: it results in the depletion of the individual's work team effectiveness, plus the cost of getting a new employee "up to speed," and re-developing and refreshing the work team. Added to this is the costs of a new hire (estimated by SHRM in 2017 as $4,425 / person or $14,936 / Executive).

Organizations have also invested heavily in areas such as leadership development and training. The goal of these investments is to ensure a culture of collaboration, cooperation, and effective communications, leading to the building of trust and a greater level of employee engagement. This development is also aimed at avoiding unethical behaviour, unfair treatment, harassment, and other negative workplace conduct. Again, these investments are rarely tracked, nor is the sustainability of them and their ongoing effectiveness reported.

Organizations have also invested heavily in areas of inter-personal skills, including developing skills such as structured problem resolution so as to help develop, build, and sustain key relationships with third parties, such as partners in the supply chain. Again, these investments are not tracked or reported, nor is the ongoing performance and sustainability monitored. This focus on engagement has significant financial benefits. In May 2021, Willis Towers Watson published an article, *Why is employee engagement important?*[24] that identified several organization-wide improvements, such as:

> *Companies with above average employee engagement achieved profit margins five points higher than their sectors' typical results. By comparison, companies with below average employee engagement faired 13 points lower. We also saw earnings results for companies with above average engagement beat sector performance by more than two times the rate of companies with below average engagement.*

The investment made to create this environment creates a key competitive infrastructure and is part of its business model. It also drives up the value of the business to an investor. The investments have lasting benefits and human capital reporting should address both the activity required to sustain this level of engagement and the "health of the asset."

Investments create intangible infrastructure that is essential to the continued working of an organization's business model; reduction in the capacity or capability of these areas can bring significant risk to an organization. Human capital reporting needs to start filling these gaps. What must be part of populating the new reporting model?

There are two aspects that must be addressed – first what is the "value," not only in financial terms but also in other aspects of value. This is

---

[24] https://www.willistowerswatson.com/en-GB/Insights/2021/05/why-is-employee-engagement-important

important because what has been built up over the last 30 years is a major investment in these capabilities that is reflected in the investors' value of the business and in the organization's ability to "sustain operations." Secondly, because these are important "past investments," as well as a key aspect of capability moving forward, the "health" of these investments needs to also be known. Sadly, as Table 5.4 shows, currently reporting tells us little.

Table 5.4 The value that human capital creates

Aspect	Value of "the asset"	Visibility into health
Supply chain relationship	Known in terms of purchase cost / materiality but impacts operating expenses, acquisition costs, design, agility	Limited – change of supplier / turnover
Customer relationship	Known in terms of sales value, but impacts re-buy intention, brand, market ideas and innovation	Limited – turnover, exclusivity, sole source / preferred supplier
Distribution relationship	Known in value volume but impacts take to market costs, customer impact and market feedback / innovation	Limited – satisfaction / turnover, exclusivity
Workforce skill capability	Known in terms of salary and benefits cost; unknown in value	Limited – known in turnover, losses / retention, engagement
Workplace culture	Unknown other than costs committed to leadership development	Limited – source of turnover / retention, levels of innovation, creativity, disputes, discipline actions
Other relationships	Unknown but negative impact on problems and delays as a cost	Incidents, delays, problems, complaints
Knowledge base	Unknown – retained as a personal asset of the individual	Limited – related to engagement, involvement, participation on project's
Intellectual codified	Limited – cost of some acquisitions, costs related to building knowledge base	Limited – use of knowledge base, employment applications as employer of choice

While investments made in equipment remain as an identified and reported asset, there is no such ongoing reporting of these key intangibles. Supply chain relationships are a good example. Consider the considerations and processes involved in developing and maintaining supply chain relationships:

- Establishing operational supply chains creates an aspect of value (relationship capital) to an organization (that is usually reflected in its market value).
- Significant human effort is invested in creating key supply chains.
- Ongoing savings in areas such as administrative costs, design costs, support costs, as well as sustaining competitive product or service pricing, are an ongoing benefit to an organization, contributing to savings in financial capital.
- Many organizations reduce or eliminate inventory by developing supplier relationships, changing the operational risk profile of the organization.
- The payback of many relationships is more cost-effective operations, i.e., a return on investment (ROI) from investing human effort – supplier selection, systems development, internal process developments.
- A high performing supply chain will require limited consumption of human capital to sustain it, while a poorly performing supply chain will require higher levels of human interventions.
- The "value" of a supply chain can be added to or depleted by human behavior (Are we "easy to do business with?")

The health of the supply chain will impact the allocation of human capital needed to sustain it. One approach might be to link the "sunk cost" of these investments to turnover statistics, as a basis for nominal "value" reporting.

While HR, especially learning and development professionals, will be familiar with the challenge of "keeping current" and the "decay rate" of initiatives in learning, there are massive hidden costs that form part of the increasing "value" of the people who together make up the workforce. While current metrics track spending on learning and development, they provide little insight into organizational outcomes, nor is there any reporting (again) of the cumulative amounts that have been invested in the workforce and the impact of the loss of these sunk costs when people leave or are unavailable for work, or of the cumulative level of investments that underpins the value of the workforce (see Table 5.5).

Table 5.5 Investments in human capital – to acquire and develop

Investment	Impact / life of sunk costs
Talent acquisition	Costs might be collected in a pool and notionally amortized based on target turnover rate (with extra write off when turnover increases or lay-off's occur)
Orientation / onboarding costs	Could be treated as above in a pool; could also be written off over say a three year period.
Job skills development	Cumulative training could be collected in a pool by employee and amortized based on type of position or training involved
Leadership development	Part of cumulative investment cost in building and sustaining a culture; costs accumulated in pool and amortized over some period.

This would apply to the costs related to sustaining human capital. Similar approaches might be used to collect investments made to build other capitals, like supply chain relationships. While these costs would be collected by accounting, they would not become part of financial assets but would be reported as a pro-forma item support investment in human capital.

5.2.7 Embedding HR management processes

Numerous traditional human capital metrics will continue to play an important part in developing future needs. These fall into the following types:

- Functional measures that report the effectiveness of HR processes, e.g., training and development statistics.
- Organization-level measures relative to people, e.g., absenteeism, turnover.

- Organization-level "availability" numbers, e.g., workforce skills, knowledge, attributes, as well as diversity reporting.
- Operational measures that focus on areas like health and safety.
- Other mandatory compliance measures.
- Measures of work environment usually gained from surveys and other tools.

Many of these are already included in ISO 30414 and many are also creeping into additional mandatory requirements, such as SASB standards, SEC reporting and the EU requirements.

These will continue to be an important aspect of future reporting, and they will fit into various categories. As an example, many measures that are very important will fit within the segment related to HR processes. It is widely accepted that there is a key link between how internal HR processes work and how they affect employees' morale and motivation.

HR is responsible for the processes related to "sourcing" many of the people needed for the business, in the same way that accounting sources financial capital. HR also runs the "internal business" of providing HR services and is often seen as a service provider to the business units; in fact, sometimes this is enough of a separate business that some organizations decide to outsource these services (in which case performance metrics on the suppliers' processes would be equally as important but designated possibly as "service standards"). HR also has a role in ensuring that "people-related" regulations are being complied with – in the same way that accounting ensures that regulatory requirements are being met.

The next chapter on populating the proposed framework will clearly demonstrate the importance of these HR process metrics, as well as the way in which existing metrics might be used. It will also show how there may be opportunities for some organizations to significantly enhance their approaches to process management in HR by adopting operational style process development, management, and measurement approaches.

5.2.8 Human, relationship, and intellectual capitals

While there are many challenges in reporting human capital, especially within an integrated context, there are some additional core issues that need to be considered. Human capital is not owned but rented, so that the skills, competencies, capabilities, and experience that impact their productivity are owned by the people. The result is that the loss of an employee means the loss of these underlying attributes that could have benefitted the organization.

Metrics such as turnover become more critical as organizations develop and depend upon the capabilities that belong to the people / human resources. Sustaining a work environment that encourages people to join the organization, give 100% of their potential to the organization, and then stay for a reasonable length of time, become strategically critical. The inability to do this creates a competitive disadvantage, increases operating costs, and reduces engagement.

Many relationships are also heavily dependent on people in terms of activities carried out through person-to-person contact. There are many relationships that impact an organization's capabilities, for example:

- internal relationships between employees within the same department, different departments, different divisions, sections, geographies and more;
- internal relationships between employees, supervision, and management – again "one-on-one" and on a broader basis; and
- external relationships between employees and customers, suppliers, regulators, agencies, and others.

The first two of these – internal relationships – focus on the need to eliminate "silos" that reduce collaboration and coordination. Introducing more complication is the breadth of the workforce and the relationships within it. Today, not all the workforce is "on the payroll." Many are contracted, part-time or casual employees. Many may be employed by an external organization that provides products or services. Such relationships are also critical, especially when non-employees "represent the brand;" organizations may have become increasingly dependent on the knowledge, skills, and experience of people in other organizations and are at increased risk because that work environment is not under their control.

One might argue that, in the world of remote working and cyber shopping, personal relationships are becoming less important, but it was these relationships that were developed in the workplace prior to the Covid-19 pandemic, that enabled the online world of work to operate during times of "lockdown". A return to work will probably be important to reinforce these connections.

These challenges of reporting on the knowledge, skills, capabilities, and competencies of human relationships raise the issue of how to report human capital. Should knowledge, skills, experience, capabilities, and competencies be reported as part of human capital or as intellectual capital? Given that it is only "separated from the individual" once it has been codified or shared, this might be the basis of reporting. Intellectual capital reflects what the organization has codified and made explicit, while the remainder is an attribute of the "quality and capability" of the workforce.

Many organizations understand this challenge in terms of "intellectual capital," which they seek to protect as an organizational asset. Hence, legal aspects, such as non-disclosure agreements and non-compete clauses, have become so important. This underlying "human knowledge" might be thought of as the "lubricant" that allows an organization to operate. Again, one might argue that the development of Artificial Intelligence (AI) is decreasing the importance of human relationships and dependence on human capital, but there will always be a portion of human activity and interaction that is personal.

A very recent development is a proposal in Ontario, Canada, to introduce legislation to forbid employee non-compete clauses. As reported in the *Globe and Mail* (October 25, 2021)[25], *"The Ontario government introduced legislation on Monday that would ban the practice of imposing non-compete clauses on employees, a growing trend that the province's Labour Minister says is often used to intimidate workers."*

This need for collaboration and cooperation in an IT intensive business and what can happen when relationships are not functioning effectively, is illustrated in the book *The Phoenix Project*[26]. It is the wealth of human talent that brings its knowledge, skills, and experience to the workplace and applies these to "get the work done." This is the "value" of human capital. However, there is a degree of risk in making this happen that depends on the level of cooperation and collaboration.

The Figure 5.14 illustrates some key points for consideration of both the scope and breadth of human capital and its general relationship to intellectual capital. It can also be seen from the figure that this human capacity / capability is a driver of value creation, whether it remains tacit (in the heads of the people), has been shared with others (making it "common knowledge,") or is explicit (having been converted in patents, trademarks, license agreement, or documented). Note that the greatest risk exists when knowledge is tacit rather than codified or explicit (bottom of the chart).

---

[25] https://www.theglobeandmail.com/canada/article-ontario-to-propose-ban-on-non-compete-clauses-for-employees/
[26] Kim, Gene, Behr, Kevin, and Spafford, George, *The Phoenix Project: A Novel About IT, Development Ops, And Helping Your Business Win*, 2018, IT Revolution.

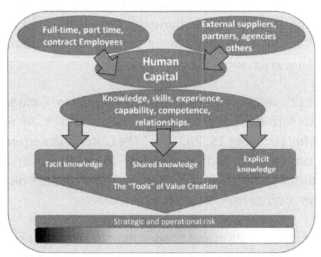

Figure 5-14 Total human capital and its "intellectual capability"

Although human capital has become a "tool of value creation," it has also become a major risk in assessing organizational resilience or sustainability. It is material to the well-being and capacity of the organization, both in terms of "talent" *and* in terms of the work climate: *both* are key aspects of "system capability and value" that investors are willing to pay for. This is because much of the output and outcome of human capital effort is the creation of "invisible assets" for the organization.

One only has to look at the vast sums of money provide by venture capitalists and Initial Public Offerings (IPOs), and consumed during development and start-up of technology-based organizations, to realize that this money was used to build infrastructure upon which future revenues are to be generated.

The case of Uber may be an extreme one; it employs about 23,700 people globally, most of whom are involved in research and development, sales and marketing, and administration. Revenue per employee is about $500K, but – in 2020 – losses were running at about $272,000 per employee. The revenue is earned by a high number of independent drivers estimated to be between three and four million; in 2020 it was estimated that there were 93 million active users on the system, and these users took an estimated 1.44 billion trips.

The relatively small number of employees do not directly create revenue but they enable and support the infrastructure on which the whole business operates. Traditional revenue / employee metrics would be of limited value in this case. The real value in Uber is the capability of the system (infrastructure), the value of the customer network (existing and other users), the brand (valued at approximately $5B in 2020) and presumably the effectiveness with which the people work together. This last point may stir a good debate about culture metrics given some of the swings in valuation of Uber related to marketplace problems dating back several years (many of which relate to "culture" and workplace health / quality). What types of human capital metrics would demonstrate the value generated by the people employed by Uber? In 2018, there were apparently 1,300 patents applied for and 904 issued. Where is the human outcome reflected in terms of intellectual capital reflected in this reporting?

There is clearly a growing need to understand the link between human performance and the generation of value in terms other than revenues or profits. This is the challenge of understanding and communicating *value* in terms of *outputs* and *outcomes* in areas that are not clearly visible through traditional reporting. It will also be important to determine how human capital is being deployed to sustain these aspects of organizational value that contribute to an investor's value, and which is far greater than that reflected in traditional financial and human metrics reporting.

Integrated human capital reporting – summary
• Human capital is one of six capitals in an integrated business model.
• The collective capitals form the basis of the inputs, activities, outputs, and outcomes aspects of business model.
• Human capital consumes a large part of financial capital and is also the way cash is converted into other capitals.
• Integrated reporting requires changes in the way all four aspects of the business model are reported.
• Integrated reporting requires human capital to be thought about from five perspectives: financial, operational, work environment / culture, good governance, and HR management.
• The work of people has changed, so activities must reflect both current and strategic outputs and outcomes.
• Human capital must be approached using a PDCA framework – Plan, Do, Check and Act.
• All HR metrics must be linked to organizational goals and objectives.
• Talent works best through an effective culture
• Productivity (activity) metrics must be separated into operational performance and quality of work environment.
• International guidance and standards are emerging for effective human capital structure and leadership.
• The visibility between human capital / effort and the creation / sustaining of intangibles must be evident.

Integrated human capital reporting – checklist
• Is human capital (the "people" side of the business) considered equivalent to other capitals?
• Does organizational level strategic thinking and planning drive all aspects of human capital?
• Are all human capital metrics aligned with assessing progress against planned goals and activities?
• Is the link between financial capital (investment) and human activity clearly demonstrated?
• Is the quality of the work environment being measured to assess the "enablement" of human potential?
• Is decision making aimed at optimizing both organizational performance and the sustainability of *all* capitals?
• Are human capital metrics aligned with the business model aspects of input, activity, output, and outcome?
• Are there clear, non-financial human capital goals and outcomes?
• Are human capital metrics being developed under the five core aspects of financial, operational, culture, good governance and HR process management?

Human Capital Metrics

6 Choosing metrics for the model

6.1 Developing metrics with meaning and value

Now that we have a framework that reflects the key steps in the business model – input, activity, output, and outcome – and a series of groupings which contain different aspects of human capital as a key business resource, the next step is to start populating it with individual metrics. The key goals in developing specific metrics must be to ensure that:

- **outcome** metrics can be clearly linked to organizational goals and objectives;
- human capital planning has adequately aligned desired outcomes to organizational **activities** and **outputs**; and
- performance expectations have been established against which the activities and outputs can be measured and monitored.

Using this approach, the desired outputs and outcomes can be directly linked to the management of day-to-day activities through which people deliver results. Only by this clear connection will the necessary metrics be developed and created, and a linkage to action and decision-making established to ensure the desired outcomes; and if these are not "on track," what specific activity or group of activities, needs to be addressed.

In the first part of this chapter, we will look at how to start populating the model with metrics that may already be known and available. Following this, the challenge of developing alignment and "roll up" of core high-level outcome metrics will be discussed and, finally, the way forward on human resource activity management will be covered.

6.2   Metrics for populating the new model

There are many sources of potential human capital metrics to choose from. These have been covered in earlier chapters of the book but include GRI, SASB, WEC and others. ISO 30414:2018 has also been discussed and, for the purposes of building an integrated reporting approach, this will be used as the foundation. Building and populating the model will be done in phases.

Before the metrics are chosen, it is recommended that readers review the guidelines for applying integrated reporting published by the IIRC / Value Foundation and the ISO 30414:2018 standard. Both include important steps in determining what metrics are relevant to each unique organization. These documents also explain considerations relative to scope, materiality, and other basic assumptions. There are essentially three questions to ask in determining metrics to populate the reporting model:

What metrics do we have?
What type are they are where do they fit?
What else do we need to know?

The external reporting metrics recommended in the ISO 30414:2018 guideline provide a good starting point, so this will be an answer to the first question (full details of how to select, calculate and apply these metrics are included in the standard). In the information presented here (and in Table 6.1), only the titles of metrics are given; these are in wide use and generally accepted within the HR community. Readers should consult both ISO 30414:2018 and the supporting technical specifications, which provide full detail of the metrics and how to calculate them. In the following tables, the last four columns are headed I, A, O, O, representing Input, Activity Output and Outcome, respectively.

6.2.1 Are metrics comprehensive?

Using the Input – Activity – Output – Outcome framework, and the five "types" of metrics, the second question, "where might these items best fit?" needs to be addressed. Further, what do the metrics on compliance and ethics tell us about the performance of the business model? Once these two points have been addressed, that leaves the questions "What else is needed? and are all aspects of planning and execution being reported?"

CLUSTER	SUGGESTED EXTERNAL METRIC	I	A	O	O
Compliance and ethics	• Number and type of grievances filed • Number and type of concluded disciplinary actions • Percentage of employees who have completed training on compliance and ethics				
Costs	• Total workforce costs				
Diversity	• Diversity relative to age, gender, disability, other • Diversity of leadership team				
Leadership	• Leadership trust				
Culture					
H&S and Well-being	• Lost time injury • Number of occupational accidents • Number of people killed during work				
Productivity	• EBIT / Revenue / turnover / profit per employee • Human Capital ROI				
Recruitment, mobility and turnover	• Average length of time to fill vacant positions • Average length of time to fill critical vacant positions • % of positions filled internally • % of critical positions filled internally • Turnover rate				
Skills and capabilities	• Total development and training costs				
Succession planning					
Workforce availability	• Number of employees • Number of full time equivalents				

Table 6-1 Suggested external reporting metrics included in ISO 30414:2018

First, each of the clusters in Table 6.1 will be discussed as to their relevance and "fit;" Table 6.2 shows the completed table indicating whether the metrics are input, activity, output or outcome. This is not an exact science and healthy debate about where metrics fit is encouraged!

All three of the metrics in the "Compliance and ethics" grouping tell us what happened as an output of the system. Looking at "number and type of grievances filed," this is an output of the activities that take place in the workplace. The outcome might be "lower employee engagement" or "higher turnover" – or even "decline in reputation."

The metric for the next group, "Costs," is again an output; it reflects the number of financial resources committed to human activity in the conversion process. Financial capital has been converted to human capital and this is the metric of resource consumption. Again, it is not an outcome.

The next grouping may be a bit more complicated and open to discussion. "Diversity" (and inclusion) are related to "what we have" in terms of the available workforce; diversity is also a metric of the result of the hiring process. Therefore, it might be used as either an input or an output metric. Interestingly, if it is an output in the sense of being the result of the hiring process, that would also be an input as the "starting point" for the next cycle.

The suggested metric for the "Leadership" grouping – Leadership trust – is an outcome of the activities that take place in the organization. One might argue that it is an outcome but, in all probability, trust is just one factor within an overall outcome – such as lower turnover or higher employee engagement – each of which is the result of a combination of activities and processes. The next metric is one that many organizations will already be using.

Again, under "H&S and Well-being," the three external metrics are the result of – or output from – activity taking place. The outcomes of these items might be more negative workplace insurance ratings, or a reduction in reputation leading to decline in attractiveness as an "employer of choice."

"Productivity" is a well-established metric but, in all cases, it is a composite metric of system performance – not an outcome. (It is also a proxy measure for human capital because HC-ROI performance can improve with no changes being made to human capital management.) Again, the outcome measures of "human capital metrics expressed in financial terms" would be market value, credit ratings, dividends paid – not things that are a *direct* result of the activities but an overall outcome from the effectiveness of the system in meeting goals and objectives.

"Recruitment, mobility, and turnover" is, again, a well-established group of metrics – but what are they telling us? The first two items can be classified as activity, as they are identifying process performance. The next two metrics can be considered output measures, as they are demonstrating a result of the activity or process. Finally, turnover rate – one of the most important metrics in human capital – can be an output because it measures the combined success of all human capital activities, but it is more appropriate to be an outcome because it is an aggregated measure of system's effectiveness. However, one might argue that the *real outcome of turnover* would be higher costs (using more financial capital than need be), a depletion of human and intellectual capital, and possibly a decline in social / relationship capital leading to more challenges in hiring.

The "Skills and capabilities" grouping again represents a well-established human capital metric, albeit one that is widely misused. While it might be an indicator of effective management of human capital, as is often suggested, there is no clear correlation between what is spent on training and development and the effective use of human capital. Nor is there a clearly demonstrated link between organizational value and sustainability (resilience) and the spending. What it tells us is the financial amount spent on training, i.e., the amount of financial capital consumed in the activity of training people; it is therefore an output.

The last external reporting group of metrics of ISO 30414:2018 is "Workforce availability". This is similar to the earlier discussion; it measures availability of input for the process, as well as an output at the end of the process, including the results of hiring and other human capital processes that either add to or remove the availability of human capital.

Table 6-2 Suggested external reporting metrics from ISO 30414:2018 assigned to Input, Activity, Output, and Outcome (I, A, O, and O, respectively)

GROUPING	SUGGESTED EXTERNAL METRIC	I	A	O	O
Compliance and ethics	• Number and type of grievances filed			X	
	• Number and type of concluded disciplinary actions			X	
	• Percentage of employees who have completed training on compliance and ethics			X	
Costs	• Total workforce costs			X	
Diversity	• Diversity relative to age, gender, disability, other	X		X	
	• Diversity of leadership team	X		X	
Leadership	• Leadership trust			X	
Culture					
H&S and Well-being	• Lost time injury			X	
	• Number of occupational accidents			X	
	• Number of people killed during work			X	
Productivity	• EBIT / Revenue / turnover / profit per employee • Human Capital ROI			X	
Recruitment, mobility and turnover	• Average length of time to fill vacant positions		X		
	• Average length of time to fill critical vacant positions		X		
	• % of positions filled internally		X		
	• % of critical positions filled internally		X		
	• Turnover rate			X	X

Readers might note that two of the groups of metrics within ISO 30414:2018 are not included above: "Culture" and "Succession planning." There are no identified metrics in these two categories for external reporting. This may seem strange, but it should be considered part of the evolution in thinking about what is needed to assess performance of "the whole system."

In the case of "Culture", metrics to evaluate this aspect of organizational performance are in the early development stage. In the ISO technical specification, two key aspects are identified. First, employee turnover and employee retention are both "system indicators" of cultural fitness or health; thus, these may be seen as an outcome of whole system performance. Second, it is suggested that a series of assessments is needed to assess overall culture, and such approaches are at a very early stage; in many cases, they are organization specific and a challenge to benchmark. While "Succession planning" has no defined external reporting metrics, it does have five that are suggested for internal use which will be discussed later. Here are the results of the discussion in input, activity, output, and outcome.

Looking at this summary of the external metrics and their grouping into the four categories (Table 6.2), indicates that there are many output metrics but very few measures of outcome. This is clearly an issue that will need to be developed further if the importance of human capital to organizational strategy, goals, and objectives is to be taken into account.

This list of metrics also starts to raise the discussion about what should be disclosed externally versus used internally. This question of how deep to go with external metrics will be a constant challenge. The guidance on disclosure included as part of frameworks such as GRI and IIRC (Value Foundation, Integrated Reporting Framework) provide a good base of guiding principles. The following key aspects are extracted from page 7 of the January 2021 International <IR> Framework:

- (Link to) Strategic focus and future orientation.
- (Demonstrate) Connectivity of information.
- (Identify) Stakeholder relationships.
- (Reflect) Materiality.
- Conciseness.
- Reliability and completeness.
- Consistency and comparability.

These guiding principles clearly support earlier discussions relative to *outcomes* as they link both to strategy and to risk related to future capability. The other principles provide help in building a series of metrics that deliver value to the users of the information. The last three items may be seen as aspirational by some, but they are goals for the evolution of metrics that can eventually allow users to rely upon and apply the information.

The next step is to review the list of guiding principles, together with the metrics, and see where each might fit in the five different aspects or groups. Again, this is not an absolute exercise but more a process of trial and error to develop an "integrated thinking model" and approach.

Note that, in Table 6.3, the numbering shows operational management and leadership of human resources as 2A and 2B, primarily because in most traditional metrics related to human performance the impact of culture and leadership on operational effectiveness is seen as one item. This creates a problem as the underlying culture is a driver of overall workplace effectiveness. Assessing and monitoring the quality of the workplace will create enhanced understanding of performance and will provide better linkages for action. This type of metric will go a long way to supplementing and even replacing surveys.

Table 6-3 The five aspects or types of human capital reporting

Aspects of resource / capital management	Input	Activity	Output	Outcome
1. Financial investment in human resources. Goal - understand cash flow investment in people (managing the "asset" that is invested in)				
2A. Operational management of human resources Goal - effective management (use) of human resources				
2B. Leadership of human resources Goal - sustaining optimum climate for human resources				
3 "Good Governance" Goal compliance, social responsibility, and optimum talent pool				
4. HR management Goal - effective operation of HR processes				

Some of the metrics already discussed will be used as examples of "best fit," starting with compliance and ethics (cf. Table 6.2):

GROUPING	SUGGESTED EXTERNAL METRIC	I	A	O	O
Compliance and ethics	• Number and type of grievances filed			X	
	• Number and type of concluded disciplinary actions			X	
	• Percentage of employees who have completed training on compliance and ethics			X	

"Compliance and ethics" metrics are indicators of the "risk climate" relative to unplanned actions by people. It also indicates behavioral issues that might be present and, therefore, may link with leadership and culture. While the training metric does provide insight into risk, it is probably a "best fit" in terms of the effectiveness and coverage of the HR functional processes. (It would be better to ask: Why have more people not been trained?) Thus, we can start to populate our categories or aspects with existing items (cf. "aspects" in Table 6.3):

ASPECT	INPUT (I)	ACTIVITY (A)	OUTPUT (O)	OUTCOME (O)
Financial investment				
Operational management				
Cultural (Leadership)			• Number and type of grievances filed • Number and type of concluded disciplinary actions	
Governance (Social responsibility)				
Functional - HR process management			• Number of employees who have completed training on compliance and ethics	

Another example could be drawn from the "Recruitment, mobility, and turnover" cluster (cf. Table 6.2):

GROUPING	SUGGESTED EXTERNAL METRIC	I	A	O	O
Recruitment, mobility and turnover	• Average length of time to fill vacant positions		X		
	• Average length of time to fill critical vacant positions		X		
	• % of positions filled internally			X	
	• % of critical positions filled internally			X	
	• Turnover rate			X	X

The best fit for the first four metrics would be as activities and outputs of the HR processes, since HR is responsible for the recruitment process, and clearly a measure of the time to fill vacancies is a reflection on how well the process is working. The next two metrics are suggested as outputs from the activity or process of hiring. The final metric, turnover, is *not* an HR process issue but falls into more of an "enterprise wide" composite metric.

ASPECT	INPUT (I)	ACTIVITY (A)	OUTPUT (O)	OUTCOME (O)
Financial investment				
Operational management				
Cultural (Leadership)				
Governance (Social responsibility)				• Turnover
Functional - HR process management		• Average length to fill vacancies • Average length to fill critical vacancies	• % of positions filled internally • % of critical positions filled internally	

Turnover is a very broad, enterprise-wide governance metric (that might be "Cultural" also), and it might be argued that "% of positions filled internally" is not a "pure" activity measure but a composite measure of both the effectiveness of the process and the effectiveness of other activities. As an example, if the approach / activity of "succession planning" is not working well, this would directly contribute to problems in filling vacant positions internally. Another factor affecting turnover might be poor reputation.

6.2.2   Broadening the metric pool

To present a more complete picture of what the suggested framework of metrics might look like when populated, more items can be added to the shortlist discussed above (Table 6.3), which only looked at the external reporting metrics suggested in the ISO standard.

Another source of potential metrics, already in broad use, is the GRI, a short extract of which is given in Table 6.4. These selected metrics are from the larger list shown in Chapter 3 (Table 3.1), in which all the key GRI metrics related to human capital are listed.

Table 6-4 An example of some GRI metrics that might fit the reporting model

	SOCIAL TOPICS	I	A	O	O
401-1	New hires and turnover by age group, gender and region		X	X	
401-2	Benefits provided to full time employees		X		
401-2	Parental leave entitlement, use and return to work		X		
402-1	Notice (termination) time periods, union and non-union		X		
403-1	Information on Occupational Health and Safety management system(OHS)		X		
403-2	Hazard identification, risk assessment and incident investigation		X		
403-3	Occupational health services provided		X		
403-4	Worker participation, consultation and communication on OHS		X		
403-5	Training on occupational health and safety			X	
403-6	Promotion of worker health		X		
403-7	Prevention and mitigation of occupational health and safety impacts linked by business relationships		X	X	
403-8	Workers covered by an occupational OHS management system	X			
403-9	Information on work related injuries		X		
403-10	Information on work-related ill health		X		

This (400 series) group of metrics is considered by GRI as "Social Disclosures." While many of them link to "societal" outcomes, they also focus on what processes are in place to support and protect people. These can provide a rich source of ideas about how to populate a human capital scorecard.

To enhance this list, organizations can add from other sources, such as local compliance and reporting requirements. Each organization will have its own "Purpose" that sets the foundation for its business activities, and a set of defined "Values" that guide "the way we do things around here." These will drive unique strategies within the business model which, in turn, will create the need for specific metrics. Depending upon location, there will also be mandatory compliance metrics that should be included. A great example of how these types of "local metrics" combine with general metrics is demonstrated by draft legislation in the USA for possible SEC reporting. The following items would clearly only be applicable to US organizations:

- the total dollar value of assessed fines under the Occupational Safety and Health Act of 1970;
- the total number of actions brought under section 13 of the Occupational Safety and Health Act of 1970 to prevent imminent danger; or
- the total number of actions brought against the issuer under section 11(c) of the Occupational Safety and Health Act of 1970.

Many jurisdictions, such as the European Community, already have significant requirements in areas of human rights reporting. These can also be embedded. The various suggested metrics from the SASB (Sustainability Accounting Standards Board – now part of the Value Foundation) can also be usefully added to the list. Currently, the SASB standards address three issues related to human capital management:

- employee health and safety;
- employee diversity, inclusion, and engagement; and
- labor practices.

The SASB also has an ongoing project to expand its human capital standards, and address items including workforce composition, workforce costs, and workforce turnover. As organizations become more sensitive to societal needs related to employment, some of the metrics will start to link with items such as the UN SDGs.

There are many metrics that can be developed and added to the "Aspects" column of the new human capital reporting matrix; some examples are shown in the following that may supplement, support or even duplicate items already discussed. The metrics in Table 6.5 would focus on input type measures relative to the operational readiness of the workforce.

Grouping	Metrics
Workforce	Total number of employees Employees by position / qualification Male / female / another category Full time / part time Contract availability Retiree availability Average years of service Age distribution Availability (% of each type available) Tenure / experience / years in role Management span Direct to indirect employee ratio
Compensation	Average pay / pay grade Average pay / classification Average pay / classification as % of market Average benefit cost / person / grade / other Total payroll as % total cost

Table 6-5 Example of additional workforce and compensation metrics

It is typical that there is usually no shortage of ideas about *what* to measure; the major challenge is *why*. The impact of creating any measure in terms of consuming organizational resources can be significant; but it can also end up being demotivating if data is being collected and published that leads neither to any causal aspect nor to any change as a result. This is where "critical few" becomes important, as well as the discussion about goals and objectives for human resource management. Many metrics might measure underlying aspects of HR system performance, but others may be just "facts" – interesting but little else.

In the above example, the metrics focus on quantity. The next group is more about content, or quality, which would also be a critical element of input in terms of availability (Table 6.6). It is important to note that, to be of value, any metric in the list must be there for a purpose – either there is a goal against which it is being measured or there is an ongoing activity that needs to be monitored.

Table 6-6 Additional metrics for qualifications and diversity

Grouping	Metrics
Qualification / experience	Progress to plan (what people at what level) Years of experience Orientation completed Mandatory training completed Training up to date (i.e., current) Investment in training / person (less amort.) % managers below required performance level % managers ready for promotion % managers ready for promotion as % vacancies % key roles with identified successors ready % key roles with no successor identified
Diversity / inclusion	% achievement of statutory requirements Visible minority % employed vs. local population % management position staffed by women % management positions staffed by minorities

Notice that several of these additional metrics expand upon items already included in approaches mentioned previously, such as ISO 30414:2018; several start to "drill down" into areas that might be clear areas for action, especially where goals have been established. While the ISO metrics are related to % of people having completed training in certain areas, further metrics might be of value. For example, do all managers have a development plan? Are these plans on track? Are there any key positions with no succession plans in place?

In the next grouping (Table 6.7), the areas of both culture (the effective workplace) and risk related to human capital for stakeholders are being added. While some of these metrics are in new and evolving areas and will need experimentation, many others are items already in practise within organizations. The proposed reporting framework identifies leadership /

culture / employee engagement as a critical issue and there are many developing metrics to support these items. Some practitioners dislike approaches such as 360° assessments for individuals in management positions but these can be of value.

Table 6-7 Additional metrics for engagement, culture, and risk

Grouping	Metrics
Culture / climate	Employee engagement (or equivalent) score Net promoter scores % employees scoring managers above 80% % Trust rating % employees support / aligned with purpose Rating of total employees to organizational values Rating of managers to organizational values % External confidence / trust in organization % employees who would recommend friends Engagement rate in social activity % employees volunteering to sponsored events
Risk	% key employees with <80% satisfaction score # or % key employees eligible for retirement Of the above % with "ready successor" # key contract positions terminating within 12 months Absenteeism trend by cause # / trend of labor disputes # / % of disciplinary actions - trend

Readers should also refer to the ISO Technical Specifications that support many of the key metrics; as an example, ISO/TS 24178:2021 *Human Resource Management — Organizational Culture Metrics Cluster*, explains in detail how organizations might approach developing metrics for assessing culture. An upcoming guideline and technical specification on employee engagement will also provide help and support.

Finally, we can return to the suggested internal metrics within the ISO 30414:2018 guidance document. To date, the focus has been on external reporting, but this document has significant additional metrics that can be used internally.

These internal metrics are presented in the same groupings or clusters as the external metrics discussed already (see Table 6.1); in two cases – culture and succession planning – there were no external metrics suggested. Practitioners will know that the development of many human capital metrics can be subjective but, as human capital is increasingly seen as a key aspect of strategic competitive advantage, the development of metrics of multiple types – qualitative, quantitative, and trends – will be required. The clusters in the internal categories are listed in Tables 6.8– 6.10.

The same exercise of determining whether these items are inputs, activities, outputs, or outcomes (I, A, O, and O, respectively) will need to be followed; these items can then be added to the "pool" of possible metrics available for use.

Note that here, "Diversity" and "Productivity" have no specific internal reporting role suggested; the recommended metrics are in the external reporting area. However, it is inconceivable that these aspects of organizational activity would not in some way be included internally. Current research indicates that there is a clear link between diversity and performance; studies in areas such as financial services reveal clear competitive advantages to a diverse workforce. There would also be *major* internal expectations for productivity metrics relative to human capital for internal use.

Table 6.8 Suggestions for internal reporting from ISO 30414:2018 – first clusters

CLUSTER	SUGGESTED INTERNAL METRIC	I	A	O	O
Compliance and ethics	• Disputes referred to external parties				
CLUSTER	**SUGGESTED INTERNAL METRIC**	I	A	O	O
Recruitment, mobility and turnover	• Number of qualified candidates per position • Quality of hire • Transition and future workforce capabilities assessment (talent pool) • Percentage of critical business positions • Percentage of vacant critical positions in relation to all vacant positions • Internal mobility rate • Employee bench strength • Voluntary turnover rate (without retirement) • Voluntary critical turnover rate • Involuntary critical turnover rate • Exit / turnover reasons / leaving employment by reason				
	training				
Productivity					

Table 6.9 Suggestions for internal reporting from ISO 30414:2018 – Recruitment, mobility, and turnover

While it was suggested that "Turnover" (included as an external metric) be added in the "good governance" category, users could also either create a new area for purely compliance metrics or change the "good governance" heading to "enterprise-wide." There are many alternatives – key to the decision will be ensuring that the items within a particular area are relevant.

Clearly enterprise-wide metrics would not fall into the HR process category. Using the "Recruitment, mobility, and turnover" list (Table 6.9), the organization-level turnover number can be further broken down into areas that are more critical in terms of internal management. While "good governance" suggests that overall turnover be reported, to manage the issue internally requires drilling down into narrower detail. Also, from a risk perspective, boards (as a minimum) would want to know the risk associated with critical positions.

The final clusters (Table 6.10) rounds out the groupings of internal measures suggested in the ISO guidelines.

Table 6.10 Suggestions for internal reporting from ISO 30414:2018 – final clusters

CLUSTER	SUGGESTED INTERNAL METRIC	I	A	O	O
Skills and capabilities	• % Of employees who participate in trainings compared with total number of employees per year • Average formalized training hours per employee • % Of employees who participated in formalized training in different categories • Workforce competency rate				
Succession planning	• Succession effectiveness rate • Successor coverage rate • Succession readiness depth: ready now • Succession readiness depth: ready in 1 – 3 years • Succession readiness depth: ready in 4 – 5 years				
Workforce availability	• Contingent workforce: independent contractor • Contingent workforce: temporary • Absenteeism				

Earlier, the challenges with monitoring the recruitment activity or process were discussed and it was suggested that a poor process result could be due to poor performance in succession planning; the above metrics would be a good example of how internal monitoring would provide the information needed.

Having created a large pool of potential metrics for the reporting framework, the discussion can now return to populating the "types" of metrics into input, activity, output, and outcome categories, as well as one of the five groupings or "aspects" suggested in Table 6.3.

6.2.3   Populating the five "aspects"

Now we have started to create a larger portfolio of possible metrics, these can be inserted in the various locations within the framework. One of the benefits of going through this process is to identify what type of additional information is needed to "round out" the story that needs to be told – whether about the success that management is enjoying through the effective management of human capital or about the potential risks that may exist because this particular resource is not operating at optimum potential.

Using the external metrics discussed earlier and adding in the internal, the matrix can be updated to illustrate what breadth and depth of information is being provided.

Starting with the "Financial" aspect (see Table 6.11): there are limited financial metrics, none of which shows the scale of investment in "people" resources or what they are doing. As an example, "Cost per hire" is used as a metric but the cost disappears in the financial statements under "current operating costs." There is an item in the output category – "cost of turnover" – but there is limited correlation between the two. When a workforce extends to thousands of employees, the cost of hiring is a significant "sunk cost," and a small change in turnover rate can have a large impact on operating expenses.

Table 6.11 Existing metrics under the financial aspect of capital management

ASPECT	INPUT (I)	ACTIVITY (A)	OUTPUT (O)	OUTCOME (O)
Financial investment Investment in human resources. Goal - understand cash flow investment in people (managing the "asset" that is invested in)	• Cost per hire • Recruitment costs	• Ratio of basic salary and remuneration	• Turnover costs • Total developing and training costs • Total workforce costs • External workforce costs • Total costs of employment	

Some key questions alluded to earlier would be:
- How much accumulated "sunk cost" has been expended to hire the workforce? *This is an asset – is it being protected?*
- How much sunk cost has been expended in the structured orientation of new hires? *This is also a significant investment that has been made using financial capital.*
- How much current operational expenditure is being invested in developing intangibles versus creating current revenue producing outputs? *This is currently aggregated in financial reports and even the proposed HR metrics only show total cost of payroll / compensation, which is at too high a level, and no longer of great value.*
- What is the spending level on developing and sustaining "workplace culture"? Is the organization directing resources to build and strengthen its human capital? *Again this is an investment to enhance human capital.*
- What are the current costs of poor culture? What fees and penalties have been paid because of behavioral / ethical issues? How much is being spent on workforce conflict resolution and problems? *Only if the costs of poor culture are known will an organization be able to calculate its ROI (Return on Investment) on taking preventative actions.*

These are only a few of the possible items needed. Developing the financial aspects for future reporting should accomplish several goals.

1. Related to INPUT: Enhance the understanding of what investment has already been expended on building the human capital, which – under accounting rules – is written off as an expense.
2. Related to ACTIVITY: Develop insight into the assignment of cash flow to funding human capital, especially the amount buried in current operating (period) costs related to:

    a. building external relationships, (supply chain, customers, and others);

    b. enhancing internal effectiveness (building human capital through communications, team development and others);

    c. creating intellectual capital in terms of both tacit (investing within employee knowledge) and explicit knowledge (codifying knowledge through patents); and

    d. developing "manufactured capital" in terms of procedures, instructions, problem resolution, knowledge base creation, and others.

3. Related to OUTPUT (and linked to the various activities above): Identify the outputs that are being created from the conversion of financial capital into other capitals.

4. Related to OUTCOME: Identify the actual results delivered by the human capital relative to organizational strategy.

These are areas that need developing and on which HR and Finance need to work closely together. Some financial data may already be available depending on how costs are collected; however, some – such as accumulated costs related to areas such as training, orientation, and other items – may not be retained. These could be important aspects with respect to fully reporting the true financial implications of areas such as turnover.

The next aspect of capital management is "operational management of human resources" (see Table 6.12), which deals with the deployment of human capital within the organization. The largest portion of human capital effectiveness will relate to the workforce deployed externally to HR; metrics related to HR input, activity, output, and outcome would be reported separately in the HR aspect.

Human Capital Metrics

Table 6.12 Existing metrics under the operational aspect of capital management

ASPECT	INPUT (I)	ACTIVITY (A)	OUTPUT (O)	OUTCOME (O)
Operational management Goal - effective management (use) of human resources	• Number of employees • Full time equivalents • Contingent workforce independent contractor • Contingent workforce temporary workforce • Workforce competency rate • Employee bench strength • Percentage of critical business positions • Succession readiness rate now • Succession readiness rate 1-3 years • Succession readiness rate 4 - 5 years		• Lost time injury • Number of occupational accidents • Number of people killed during work • EBIT / Revenue / turnover / profit per employee • Human capital ROI	

Traditional metrics in this area are a high-level aggregation of total workforce costs expressed as a factor of the revenues or earnings generated. This needs to change to reflect the reality that much work is now done by people who are not on the payroll (or even employees), and a large part of the work does not relate to current revenues or profits.

Here, there appears to be a large amount of "input" information about the workforce and what is available. Using one of the earlier graphics, this would be the "pool" of resources, both quality and quantity, available to the organization that can be called upon, as required, to take part in total operational activity. This would be the labor needed for conversion of inputs to outputs. However, one major piece missing here is the assumption that most of work being done by the workforce is related to current operational activity. There is little insight into the use and deployment of people as creators of the other capitals required to sustain an organization in which relationships, intellectual capital, and workforce cohesion and capability are key competitive advantages.

From a risk perspective, as well as being an insight into the deployment of resources, this is a large gap. This also explains the lack of metrics in the activity column of Table 6.12. It is also apparent that there are no outcome metrics in the operational activity aspect. This gap may relate to the impact on society of the way in which the organization manages its human resources. While several HR metrics may already be part of operational reporting, the importance of operational deployment to the creation of intangible capital will be an important addition.

From an operational perspective, the goal of improving operational metrics would, in many ways, mirror the financial metrics just discussed; i.e., the operational metrics would be the non-financial aspects. These would include:

1. Related to INPUT: Availability aspects of strategic human / people resources - over and above the generic metrics suggested:
    a. Is there a need for further breakdown of critical positions, such as breaking out research and development?
    b. If diversity is a strategic issue (rather than compliance), could metrics focus on the input of the workforce relative to diversity against strategic goals?
    c. If the organization has an ageing population, some of the suggested metrics relative to workforce composition would be needed and, again, be compared to goals.
    d. If certain areas were short of strategic input of human capital, then these would be broken out as unique metrics – e.g., sales force available in a new geographic area.
2. Related to ACTIVITY: Many of the missing areas relate to the operational gaps mentioned in the financial segment (i.e., the financial aspects would show the consumption of financial capital into human capital, and the operational activity measures would focus on what specific activities were being undertaken).

3. Related to OUTPUT: These underpin the items discussed under the financial aspect. As can be seen in the metrics already on Table 6.12, these track traditional, generic outputs; however, as the type of work being done has changed, so have the outputs, e.g., an R&D output would be "patents filed."
4. Related to OUTCOMES: Again, this looks at non-financial outcomes and would track items like growth in the knowledge base, strength of client relationships, and other "health check" items related to the achievement of strategic goals related to intangible assets.

The next aspect is the new segment related to "culture", i.e., the work environment or work climate within which operational activities take place (see Table 6.13).

Given the importance of creating a climate within which people can contribute at their optimum level, there appear to be few metrics. The output items indicate some level of "system effectiveness" in terms of indicators of a positive or less positive work environment but provide little other information.

Maybe some growth in metrics related to input could come from the current qualification levels of supervisory staff. Maybe the existing level of employee engagement could be an input - this in effect is the opening balance of the "culture." Clearly there are many gaps in such an important aspect.

Table 6-13 Existing metrics under the culture aspect of capital management

ASPECT	INPUT (I)	ACTIVITY (A)	OUTPUT (O)	OUTCOME (O)
Cultural (Leadership) Goal - sustaining optimum climate for human resources (Focus on Culture)	• Span of control		• Turnover Rate • Exit/turnover reasons/leaving employment by reason • Voluntary turnover rate (without retirement) • Voluntary critical turnover rate • Absenteeism • Leadership trust • Number and type of grievance filed • Number and type of concluded disciplinary action • Disputes referred to external parties	

One challenge in human capital reporting is that traditional metrics combine the cultural or environmental aspects of performance management with the operational effectiveness. It provides little information about whether an organization's issue is obtaining or retaining "talent," or whether there is no problem with talent and, rather, the issue is poor leadership that is resulting in issues such as high turnover, low morale, and low productivity. With culture and people engagement becoming recognized as critical to giving a competitive advantage, more information is needed in this area. The operational aspect informed about quantity, but this is about climate or quality:

1. Related to INPUT: What is the "input climate" and is there a goal to enhance this as an outcome? Span of control is the sole input, which is an indicator of the need for control: the more effective the workforce, the less direct supervision is needed. More is needed here, which will typically come from asking: What is the opening level of aspects such as employee engagement?

2. Related to ACTIVITY: To build and sustain an effective "optimizing culture" in this new and important area, activities such as communications, coaching, mentoring, guiding, supporting, and problem solving need to take place. These should be supplemented by "non-process" activities, such as projects for team development and leadership development.
3. Related to OUTPUT: Both processes and projects would deliver results that will be part of the output.
4. Related to OUTCOMES: Here the metrics would assess the enhancement that has resulted (i.e., value created) from building the climate to enhance performance and productivity. This would mainly be in growing human capital and enhancing the value of the workforce as a strategic asset. A high-level "culture" metric would be a relevant outcome (see Chapter 7, "Measuring culture").

The development of culture metrics can replace high-level indicators, such as the amount spent in training and development, as this has limited links to strategy and tells us nothing about the work climate. As an example, the growth in employee engagement, increase in retention, growth in "employer of choice," growth in customer assessment of a "great supplier to do business with" would all be strategic outcomes.

The next category or aspect is placed on its own, as the whole area of "diversity and inclusion" is still, in many jurisdictions, something that is done because it is either a statutory requirement or is seen as "good corporate responsibility." It is, in fact just "good business." There are plenty of studies to show that, operationally, diversity is akin to enhanced talent. This is where these metrics (Table 6.14) might eventually reside.

Table 6-14 Existing metrics under the governance aspect of capital management

ASPECT	INPUT (I)	ACTIVITY (A)	OUTPUT (O)	OUTCOME (O)
Governance (Social responsibility) Goal compliance, social responsibility, and optimum talent pool	• Workforce diversity by age • Workforce diversity by gender • Workforce diversity by disability • Workforce diversity by other • Diversity of leadership team • Transition and future workforce capabilities assessment (talent pool)			

This area might also be where metrics related to an improvement in public perception around social accountability and "license to operate" – as strategic goals – would be placed. The input might be the organization's overall reputation in terms of how it is perceived by the public rather than any one group of stakeholders. There may then be activities and outputs that are designed as areas of strategic investment (converting financial capital to human capital) that have people do work related to enhancing the organization's public image. Examples could be social outreach, or charitable activities, such as staff being paid while donating time to local causes.

If an organization is investing in human capital activities to achieve these goals, then there must be metrics to support what the current position is, what the desired position should be and what activities and outputs are necessary to change from "what is" to "what should be." This aspect could also be the place to put composite metrics related to outcomes such as addressing the UN Sustainable Development Goals.

> **KEY POINT TO REMEMBER**
> ***Whatever an organization pays people to do must be linked with a purpose.*** *As more investment is made in creating and developing culture and reputation, there will be a greater need for metrics that allow these activities to be planned, implemented, and monitored effectively, the goals to be clearly established, and actual results to be compared against them. There are still big gaps in this area.*

The final of the five aspects, is the performance of the underlying human resources processes (see Table 6.15). These processes provide the operational foundation for the structural policies and programs within which people are hired, trained, paid, supported, reviewed, and a host of other underlying support areas. While leadership sets the stage for culture or climate within which people operate, the effective functioning of HR processes plays a significant role in creating a positive climate.

While some aspects of HR procedures and processes relate to the effectiveness of their operation by HR staff, the policies that the organization implements within which these take place have a profound effect on employee engagement, morale, motivation, and, through these, productivity and performance.

This is discussed at some length in my book on corporate culture[27]. One of the key failures in culture is that the "statements of intent" about "people being are our greatest asset" often fail to materialize in the eyes of the employees because HR processes fail to treat than as "the most important asset."

---

[27] Shepherd, Nick A., *Corporate Culture; Combining Values and Purpose*, 2021, , EduVision / Jannas Publications

Table 6.15 Suggested metrics for the HR aspect of capital management

ASPECT	INPUT (I)	ACTIVITY (A)	OUTPUT (O)	OUTCOME (O)
Functional - HR process management Goal - effective operation of HR processes	• Number of qualified candidates per position • Successor coverage rate • Internal mobility rate	• Average length to fill vacancies • Average length to fill critical vacancies • Percentage of vacant critical business positions in relation to all vacant positions • Percentage of employees who have completed training on compliance and ethics • Leadership development • Percentage of employees who participated in training	• Quality of hire • Learning and development: Percentage of employees who participate in training compared to total number of employee/year • Succession effectiveness rate • Percentage of positions filled internally • Percentage of critical positions filled internally • Average formalized training hours per employee • Training hours per FTE (All FTE Headcount) • Training hours per FTE (Trained only FTE Headcount) • Percentage of employees who participated in formalized training in different categories	

It is not surprising that the most heavily populated areas of human capital metrics are those related to the operations of the human resources department. This has been the traditional focus of performance management of HR and, to a degree, reflects the silo-based approach to human capital rather than the integrated system approach.

The goal must be to close the gap between what is currently available and the information about human capital that is needed to both identify the risk relative to its continued ability to support the business model, and the underlying issue of value.

Human capital is a key component in converting inputs to outputs but, as discussed, a large part of spending on people today is done to create and sustain intangible assets. This aspect of reporting is therefore critical to avoid problems in the future. It is also important that organizations create and sustain a workplace that obtains a competitive advantage from human capital. This is partly about talent management but also heavily dependent on the quality of leadership; optimizing the effective sustainability of *all* capitals is more important than maximizing profit. Finally, as society demands more from organizations in terms of the well-being of people and the society within which they live, non-financial outcomes will grow in importance. These are the outcomes in which there are gaps in human capital reporting that must be addressed; the following ideas and observations are designed to move the process forward.

6.2.4 *Human capital governance*

For many organizations, regulators, and others, much of the development of updated corporate accountability and reporting is now seen as resting under the umbrella term of ESG (environment, social and governance). It has been thought implicit that ESG reporting would include the important aspects of human capital management, yet for many organizations oversight remains incomplete in terms of the breadth of strategy necessary to become human-centric. This is probably for the following reasons:

1. The ESG movement and terminology has grown – from the triple bottom line, through corporate social responsibility (CSR) to the new integrated approaches such as <IR>.
2. During this journey, financial reporting has been a constant, but environment and social concerns have been the growth areas. Environment and, now, climate change have been heavily driven by the UN, national agendas, and the business community's response, including both investors concerned about risk (such as carbon disclosure reporting, CDR) and a growing ownership of the causes by those involved in business governance.
3. The social and environmental aspects of ESG have been strongly influenced by several business-oriented groups, as well as being impacted by growing legislation around corporate accountability.

As the societal context within which organizations operate has changed, so the pressures on Boards and others to respond have increased. These responses are expected to be demonstrated by the reporting of change and priorities in corporate governance – the "G" in ESG. Most broad-based frameworks for broader reporting and accountability, such as SASB, GRI and IIRC (now the Value Foundation), lay out expectations of a clearly demonstrated need to address *all* capitals as part of effective governance. While great progress has been made on climate change, the changes needed to address human capital and its role in strategic risk and value creation still needs more work.

First, those responsible for governance – starting at the board level – must ensure that approaches to human capital strategy view people as having an equally important role to financial capital. As already discussed, paying people consumes a large amount of financial capital. At the corporate strategy level, people have become the core resource in sustaining corporate capacity and capability – they are the owners and creators of underlying value and capability.

A heavy reliance on financial reporting obscures the resources that are being poured into the creation and sustaining of these intangibles; additionally, reliance on third-party audits to assess the health and "going concern" of a business, where over 90% of its market value rests on intangibles, is no longer an adequate assurance of the "assets" health. So, the stated approach to governance must start to reflect a people-centric, whole-system approach to oversight, which includes human capital reporting.

Secondly, governance should be critically concerned with an organization's "license to operate" in terms of the changing expectations of society. This should be the source of guidance on the metrics required for the category of human capital metrics that tell the story of the organization's impact (outcome) on society and other stakeholders, as a reflection of its social conduct. People permeate everything that happens in an organization; while many see the most important capital or resource as financial / money, the reality is that this financial capital is being converted into human capital and it is the human capital that now drives organizational capability, effectiveness, and value-creation activities; it is also the ability of an organization to retain and optimize the efforts of people that drives business risk.

Clearly, for human capital to take its place as a core resource in the new economy and be seen and reported at the level of importance that its investment and performance need, a fully "whole-system" integrated approach must be taken, which starts at the governance level.

Earlier discussions identified several key areas in which there are gaps in current approaches. *What would human capital reporting look like if investors and directors were as concerned about the impact of human capital on risk and sustainability, as they are about that of financial capital?* After almost 100 years of reporting financial capital, we have learned that we need to understand and answer the following questions:

- What was my starting capital and has this been added to or depleted during the reporting period? (In accounting terms, this would be the balance sheet).
- Why has my capital been added to or depleted during the reporting period? (Traditionally in accounting terms, this is the earnings statement).

This is a *key* pair of questions for *all* capitals. Remember, historically, financial capital represented "net worth" when it was the dominant type of capital employed. Accounting records still answer the question for financial capital, but no longer do so for the total value, as the newly introduced intangible capitals now represent a large proportion of net worth. However, the investor's question remains the same: How much capital do I have?

For human capital, the questions will also be: What do we have, how well has it been deployed, has it been enhanced or depleted, and, finally, how well was it deployed in terms of desired outcomes? In the same way that some financial capital will have considered current expense, while some is "capitalized" (e.g., buying property, plant, and equipment), so it is with human capital: some is used to generate current outcomes, and some is used to generate lasting outcomes – in effect, "intangible infrastructure." Thus, there is another question that needs to be answered: What was the "flow" of capital during the period – how much was consumed, how much was re-invested, how much was added? In effect, these are the inputs, use and outputs (what the cash flow statement traditionally presented for accounting).

This approach worked reasonably well as accounting evolved and has been fine-tuned as the financial markets changed; however, as business has shifted from deploying cash to *capital* assets to enable operations to *intangible assets*, the reliance of financial reporting has revealed gaps and risks. The goal of integrated reporting – especially reporting of human capital – should be to provide a similar level of insight into capital for report users.

The danger of becoming immersed in developing different metrics could be that one loses sight of why this is being done in the first place. It must be remembered that *any* reporting takes valuable time and resources, whether it is for internal or external use. Any metric must clearly add value for the user. However, three key things that are driving what must be reported have changed:

- the "value creation" model: this has shifted from a high proportion of tangible, "capitals" to intangibles that, while critical, are not visible;

- financial investment: resources are being heavily invested in building intangibles, which includes developing, motivating, and sustaining an effective workforce; and
- societal expectations around people and work.

How is progress to date reflecting the changed realities in these three areas? How is the transition to a new set of metrics progressing? There are clearly some key gaps in the knowledge of human capital that need to be addressed for progress to be made; we need to find ways to:

1. develop improved visibility between financial value that investors are willing to pay for an organization and its human capital investments;
2. better understand the outputs and outcomes from the investment in human capital in terms of other capitals being created – such as social / relationship capital, manufactured capital, intellectual capital, and, possibly, natural capital;
3. more effectively identify the link between outcomes from investment in human capital and the achievement of organizational goals;
4. better identify activity, output, and (especially) outcome metrics that reflect the development of a people-centric workplace (an effective culture that optimizes human capability); and
5. better identify the link between human capital outcomes and sustainable organizational value so as to identify organizational risk.

The link to financial outcomes remains important and bears re-emphasis. *To understand the challenge of integration is to realize that the additional five capitals are not "add-on" components that are intended to drive more areas of silo-based functional reporting; they are the crystallization of management activities that have been occurring over many years, by diverting and investing financial resources into the creation of intangibles, most of which have remained invisible to investors. Not only has this created the growing gap between traditional accounting and market value it has also created "new" capitals that form part of an integrated system in combination with financial capital.*

Financial capital remains a critical one of the six capitals, but integrated reporting should reveal the degree to which investment has been shifting, new "capitals" have been built, and organizational capacity and capability are now dependent on *all* these capitals working together within a single, integrated business model.

This is at the foundation of the <IR> framework and lies behind the development of the need for reporting on all six capitals. This might best be illustrated by showing how financial capital is already being invested in the five other capitals, which are often not visible because financial reporting does not identify them. This could be part of "operational" human capital metrics; it would illustrate the deployment of human capital in both the "activities" reported and the outputs and outcomes.

6.2.5   Human metrics data variation

Some human capital data for reporting metrics will be considered as hard facts, e.g., number of employees or contractors, number of new people hired, amounts paid in payroll and benefits. However, some data will be subject to variation and the question is whether it can be relied upon.

There is obviously variation in data such as surveys, especially employee surveys that have long been used to assess employee satisfaction. This variation could be seen as a reason to downgrade such metrics as less valuable; yet, at a time when organizational climate plays a critical role in operational effectiveness, this type of feedback is more critical than ever.

Regular assessments of employee engagement and feedback on the work culture must be seen as important to track, and that will become a critical metric as part of human capital reporting. Yet, at what point should management start to become concerned about the organization's responses? Is the cultural climate still "in control?" How can variations in data be dealt with in a way that evolving issues can be identified? Certainly, the annual employee survey approach is inadequate as a data gathering tool in the rapidly changing organizational environment. Additionally having only one "data reading" on everybody at a single point in time will not be representative, since natural ebbs and flows in responses are typically human.

There may be an alternative approach. Effective process management techniques, supported by Statistical Process Control (SPC) can be readily applied to HR processes, as these are a critical underpinning of employee engagement and a positive culture. For example, a weekly assessment could be done using a sample group of employees and this data could then be used to present a current (real-time, online) scorecard (see Figure 6.1); as long as responses remained "within control," there would be no concern. In Figure 6.1, this would be readings within the *green* range. However, if readings started to move towards the upper or lower "control limits" (initially the *amber* zone and possibly the *red* zone in Figure 6.1), then further action would have to be taken to bring results back into line.

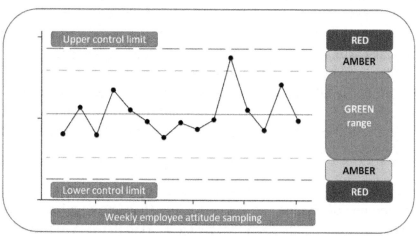

Figure 6.1 How process control and statistical process control (SPC) can be used in survey data

This approach to monitoring could also be expanded to the control of key HR processes. The technique has been adopted and effectively applied to many operational processes and is equally applicable to those that HR manages. Targets would be established for things like hiring cycle times rather than just tracking the results at completion. It would then be possible to foresee problems that might occur if process were drifting "out of control."

One critical aspect of organizational effectiveness is to create a climate that is "change ready." This gives a significant competitive advantage and is one of the goals of an effective culture. People react differently to change; creating a positive culture will enhance people's trust in, and willingness to change, although individual personalities will handle change in different ways. Therefore, one might expect a dip in the trend of culture metrics when this happens. The question is: Does the issue of culture remain within acceptable control limits? Such metrics that are somewhat subjective and demonstrate trends can be extremely valuable in assessing the health of human capital.

This has become an important aspect and is the reason why the proposed reporting model has a whole segment devoted to culture. Traditional approaches to measuring culture – using infrequent employee surveys – provide limited information at a point in time. They are also often viewed sceptically as many poor scores do not result in any changes being made. Flexibility, agility, innovativeness, "lean", and responsiveness (action-orientated) are all human qualities that provide a competitive advantage. They are all key strategic imperatives and outcomes from the business model. But if the culture is not "people sensitive," these qualities will be diminished.

As an example, let us look at a model that has been used for the management of change – a key capability that an organization needs in today's rapidly changing and evolving marketplace. A positive culture creates a much healthier environment for change because a foundation of good communications and trust has been created. The model in Figure 6.2 demonstrates the process of change within the concept of organizational

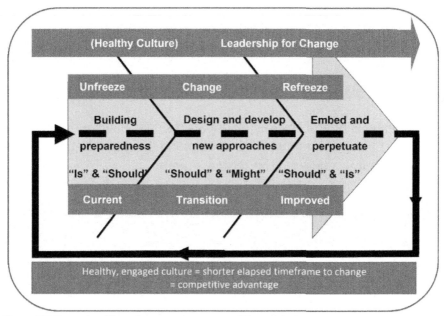

Figure 6.2 How a healthy culture creates a competitive advantage

culture. This change model is based on a well-known "Lewin" model that covers the concepts of unfreeze, change and re-freeze. All organizational change takes place in the context of an organizational culture. The length of the process is impacted not only by the complexity of the change, but also, more importantly, *by the readiness of the people to embrace the change*. This is where a positive culture provides a major competitive advantage as it reduces the time spent at all stages.

6.3   Goals, roll-up, and decomposition

Human capital metric reporting should be approached like all other areas – as an integrated aligned framework that has few measures at the strategy / high level, which can then be easily drilled down. For human capital metrics to be valuable to management and other stakeholders, they must provide information related to action. This discussion comprises the following three topics:

- linking human capital activity to organizational goals;
- setting goals for human capital and aligning these with activities; and
- grouping metrics to allow "roll-up" to high-level indicators.

Human capital is one of the key resources used to achieve organizational goals, so a starting point must be to understand the goals. Figure 6.3 shows how all six capitals underpin the business model.

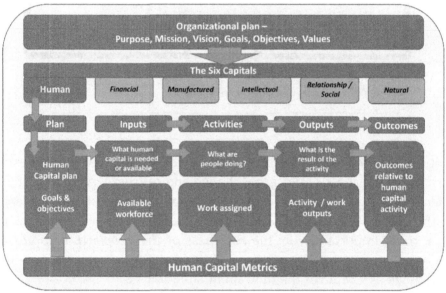

Figure 6.3 How all capitals underpin the business model

The high level "intents" of the organizational plan are only converted into reality by the integrated use of the six capitals, one of which is human capital. As part of corporate planning, the question should be: What is the human capital plan? This will translate into: What people are needed; when; and with what qualifications? (Note that this may also be where human capital supports relationship capital as well as intellectual capital). But this is only part of the plan (remember the PDCA model, Figure 5.10).

From this plan will come the desired activities necessary to engage the human capital in what needs to be done to execute the plan. As this happens, outputs will be created from the various activities and processes which, collectively, will then produce outcomes in line with the desired goals and objectives. So, underpinning the whole human capital framework, there will need to be a series of metrics to assess whether the plans, activities, outputs, and outcomes are tracking against what was expected. What might this goal setting look like when applied to some metrics that have already been discussed?

Table 6.16 Example of a scorecard showing how metrics might be grouped for a composite measure

	GOAL	ACTUAL	VAR	GREEN	AMBER	RED	WEIGHT
Number of employees	4200	4120	-80		X		25
Full time equivalents	4000	3650	-350			X	5
Contingent workforce independent contractor	550	540	-10	X			5
Contingent workforce temporary workforce	260	270	-10		X		5
Workforce competency rate	85	75	-10			X	15
Employee bench strength	85%	65%	-20.00%			X	10
Percentage of critical business positions	20.00%	32.00%	60.00%		X		10
Succession readiness rate now	50.00%	60.00%	20.00%			X	15
Succession readiness rate 1-3 years	20.00%	10.00%	-50.00%			X	5
Succession readiness rate 4 - 5 years	30.00%	30.00%	0.00%	X			5
							100

Table 6.16 shows how metrics might be grouped for a composite measure. These human capital metrics may be measuring what human resources are doing in terms of underlying activities to manage and support human capital, but the composite measure will also include operational metrics related to the effective deployment of human capital in all other activities.

This might be the first grouping related to staff availability and readiness. Goals could be set for each metric and then the actual compared to the goals, possibly using acceptable ranges of variation. As an example, "number of employees" might be a key metric (see Table 6.16); any overage to the goal might be considered an unacceptable variation, while an actual number within 5% of the goal might be acceptable. In this case the shortage is 80 people; this would be in excess of the 5% acceptable but may be a "warning;" hence, there is an amber rating on the scorecard (a cross in the 'Amber' column on Table 6.16). If an upper level of 10% had been set, the scoring would become red; then the actual is only just below that number.

This group plus other metrics that relate to "workforce readiness" could be combined and a single aggregated "index" created. As an example, the last column of Table 6.16 shows weightings that might be applied to this group from which a composite high-level ,C-suite type single metric might be created. In this way, if the overall composite rating was green or even amber, it might be considered no cause for concern, but if it were red, then the next level of metrics could be looked at to identify which specific area is presenting a problem. Many software vendors already allow for this type of metric creation within their Enterprise system software (e.g., SAP ERP system); however, the core data must be capable of being collected for the metrics reporting capability to be effective.

Creating groupings that "roll up" to higher-level human capital indicators will be a judgement decision based on the metrics being used by the organization and their strategies and goals. There are various approaches.

6.3.1 ISO 30414 "clusters"

There are 11 ISO 30414 clusters, starting with "Compliance and ethics". If this approach were used, we must ask: Does combining the metrics in this cluster provide some sensible aggregated information? In this case, the answer might be no, as one metric relates to training, while the others relate more to the culture of the workplace.

6.3.2 A four quadrant scorecard approach

This approach, as suggested by Jac Fitz-enz in a 2019 AMA blog, would group metrics using human capital management activities under acquiring, maintaining, developing, and retaining.

This is a viable alternative, but would it be grouping metrics at too high a level? Would it also seem biased towards human capital metrics reflecting mainly the work of the HR department rather than the whole organization?

6.3.3 Create groupings

One could create groupings based on major business activities related to human capital:
- New workforce attraction
- Existing workforce development
- Workforce optimization (climate, culture, safety – often referred to as a "no harm workplace)
- Turnover and retention
- Good governance (ethics, compliance, diversity, new job creation)

Again, there is no right answer. But the ability to group metrics around strategically important organizational goals would be helpful and aligns with the role of human capital as a key resource.

Rather than present a portfolio of the many potential measures available, it is recommended that organizations adopt a two-phase approach. The goal should be to establish who needs what information from the stakeholder / materiality assessment and then seek high-level external measures and lower-level internal measures.

A C-suite executive will be familiar with a scorecard approach that demonstrates the health of key organizational capabilities, activities, and results. Most human capital input measures would probably fall under the first Critical Success Factor (CSF) – related to numbers, type, skills, qualifications, status, diversity and inclusion, and so on.

Table 6-17 Core questions to create metrics at each stage of the business model (CSF: critical success factor)

CSF	Question (the answers that metrics need to provide)
Capital availability	Do we have (or have access to) the workforce talent we need? (Right people, right place, right time)?
Culture / work environment	Is our work environment healthy for people to work at their optimum level of performance?
Financial resources	What financial resources do we invest in our workforce? Is this investment being "retained", "enhanced" or depleted?
Outputs	What outputs are being created from the efforts of our human capital?
Risk	What risks should be monitored related to our human capital?
Outcomes	What value is being created from our human capital? Do our activities and outputs result in the outcomes that were planned?

As a final point, there are some metrics within existing frameworks, such as ISO 30414:2018, that have very different "values" in assessing performance. In particular, there are what might be considered composite indicators because they measure the combined results of the whole system as it impacts people (see Figure 6.4).

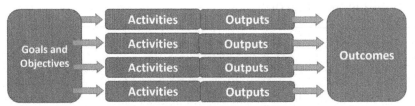

Figure 6.4 How multiple activities and outputs may be needed to convert goals to outcomes

As an example, a goal might be to enhance recruitment and talent attraction by becoming an employer of choice - or equally by being placed in the highest quartile by universities in terms of most desired employers. This would be established as a high level organization goal related to human capital. The next question is what do we have to do to achieve this?

Many activities might be involved; this may include enhancing certain recruitment processes, so they have less errors or operate at a faster cycle time. It may involve training or recruitment staff in communications skills. Each of these operational initiatives would be key to achieving the desired outcome - i.e., the goal of enhancing the appeal as an employer of choice. Metrics would be required on each of the key initiatives for operational monitoring of progress and the outcome metric would be achievement of the goal. If the goal were not achieved then using PDCA, the "Act" step would determine either which initiative was failing or a change in plans needed to reach the goal.

Composite indicators such as these will probably be seen as outcome metrics as there no direct causal link between the metric and a specific human capital activity. This is often the case where "execution" involves several activities and outputs that collectively deliver the outcomes.

The following items from ISO 30414:2018 might fall into this category. Referring to the PDCA business model, if the metrics established in Check (C) do not provide information for Act (A) to take place, they are of questionable value. Table 6.18 shows examples of high-level composite metrics within this category.

Table 6-18 Current metrics that may be considered as composite outputs or outcomes

METRIC	CONSIDERATION
Total workforce costs	Bears no direct relevance to current revenues as much of the work relates to building intangibles to create future value
Engagement / Satisfaction / commitment	High level composite indicators of an emotional "well-being" that can come from many underlying organizational and personal factors
Retention rate	Good high level indicator of overall system impact on human capital but linkages to causal factors is needed
EBIT / Revenue – turnover / profit per employee	Proxy measures of system performance of which human capital is only one input. These metrics are useful as system performance but can be misleading as a human capital indicator
Human capital ROI	As above – although data analytics have demonstrated a correlation between effective human capital management and overall system performance
Turnover rate	Good high level indicator of overall system impact on human capital but linkages to causal factors is needed
Total development and training costs	Not linked to strategic needs for capital deployment – a statement of fact similar to workforce costs. Needs linkage to outcomes.
Number of employees	Statement of fact – reveals little information about the effectiveness of human capital (or the system)

As such, these indicators can be helpful as high-level metrics but they will need "drilling down" to allow understanding of the underlying causal factors behind the numbers being reported. In developing a hierarchy and "drill-down" capability, it must be remembered that the goal is "measuring for a purpose," the most important being to be able to do something with the information.

Earlier, the role of human capital as part of the "system" was discussed, and the graphic (Figure 6.3) reflected human capital as both a critical aspect of the six capitals (resources) needed for today's business model. *Looking at the same graphic, if only <u>two</u> metrics were allowed that reflect* *the quality and leadership of human capital, they would probably be turnover and employee engagement.* While they are simplistic, these two metrics do tend to reflect the ultimate outcome of an effective approach to human capital management (see Figure 6.5).

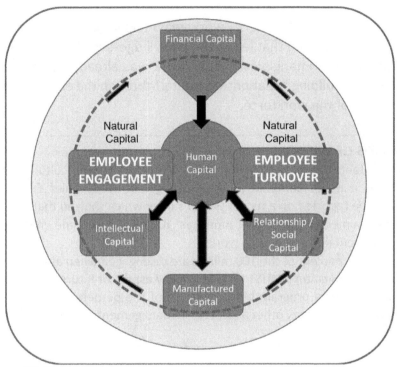

Figure 6.5 The two most important high-level composite metrics- employee engagement and employee turnover

Engagement and turnover together start to expose the foundation for the protection of human capital and the sustainability of the business model.

Understanding the importance of human capital is not new; Tom Peters, developed a loyal following as a result of his work in organizational effectiveness that culminated in the book he co-authored, *In Search of*

Excellence: Lessons from America's Best-Run Companies[28]. A core theme throughout was the importance of focus on people in an organization. At this time, business was heavily engaged in trying to improve quality and customer satisfaction, and Peters clearly demonstrated that the people in the organization were key drivers of success in these areas.

It is noteworthy that Peters' work was taking place alongside the technological evolution that led to the knowledge-based organization and the importance of intangibles. Peters' work was already focusing on the importance of building "relationship capital" through the engagement and commitment of the workforce.

WORDS OF WISDOM

Accountants cannot identify or measure the cost of poor culture, yet it creates a major competitive disadvantage. In 2019, Chief Executive magazine reported on a recent Gallup survey which showed that

- a mere 33 percent of Americas' 100 million full-time employees actually like going to work.
- 51 percent of the 100 million are disengaged when at work.

Reporting on culture MUST be a of the key aspect of future HR metrics. Culture is not a program but a measure of the perpetual climate that impacts almost every other aspect of HR management and organizational performance.

This integrated reporting model remains important and reinforces the principle that human capital is both one of the many resource inputs to a business model, and it is the operation of *the model* that creates value – not each individual capital. While the system creates value to the organization as a whole, the *key* component is people: the individual creates value by contribution to the system. People have value as individuals, but it is their collective efforts within the system that create

---

[28] Waterman, Robert H., Jr., and Peters, Tom, *In Search of Excellence: Lessons from America's Best-Run Companies, 2015, Collins Business Essentials.*

value for the organization. Trying to create a "value" for human capital as a collective asset might only work when it is recognized that it is people, together with other parts of the system that create value:

- profit drives investor attraction = financial value;
- sustainable growth drives profit growth and consistency;
- loyal customers drive sustainable revenue growth;
- engaged employees drive customer loyalty; and
- the right people in the right roles with the right managers at the right time are needed to drive employee engagement to make this work.

Many HR professionals will be familiar with the book, *First, Break All The Rules*[29]. While the book was first published over 20 years ago and now out of print, it continues to impact the Gallup Q12 report, which correlates employee engagement with organizational performance. (This Gallup report[30] should be prime reading for anyone developing HR metrics.) The opening questions suggested in the book were some of the critical few that needed to be asked to assess whether a work force was effective.

The starter questions asked about overall work satisfaction, followed by two critical questions designed to establish an individual's understanding of what was expected of them at work. This was followed by a determination as to whether the person had the needed resources to do their job; a further eight questions generated greater insight into the levels of human engagement.

This is a direct reflection of the effectiveness of the system that people work within.

---

[29] Buckingham, Marcus, and Coffman, Curt, *First, Break All The Rules: What the World's Greatest Managers Do Differently*, 1999, Gallup / Simon & Schuster.
[30] https://www.gallup.com/workplace/321725/gallup-q12-meta-analysis-report.aspx

For example, in my own experience, there have been client organizations that have very good, qualified, talented, and willing people, ready to collaborate and bring innovation to the workplace – yet their efforts are thwarted by an outdated, slow, and ineffective computer system and network. To save a few dollars on equipment, organizations waste millions in human potential. Unless the new human capital metrics start to reveal these aspects, they will add little benefit for managers and other stakeholders, because there is no clear link to causal factors or action.

A subsequent chapter will cover the breadth of a "whole-system, people-centric" approach, including the aspects that need to be addressed as part of building an effective human capital infrastructure. Importantly, still lacking in effective human capital management is a composite system-based approach that looks at how the whole HR framework is performing from an integrated system perspective. The equivalent would be using profit as a composite measure of full-system performance in the traditional sense.

While profit remains a valuable capital, it tends to focus on the effectiveness of financial capital and leaves unstated the implications of integration when financial capital is converted into other capitals. As an example, financial reports tell us whether financial capital has been depleted or enhanced in the execution of the business model but there is no report that addresses the health of human capital as a result of its involvement in the conversion process.

6.4 Bringing it all together

In the following pages, an example of a matrix has been included that shows the five separate aspects of human capital metrics together with examples of input, activity, output, and outcome measures. Some of these measures may not be applicable and it is certainly not suggested that an organization should want to adopt many of them. The aim is to show the kind of thinking from which an organization can develop its own approach to a series of metrics that can be used to populate information required for an integrated report. It is not complete. Certain metrics are shown as PTG, meaning Performance to Goal is an outcome measure, indicating that each organization would use this idea for a metric relative to a goal or objective that is unique to that organization. The matrix should be considered as a work in progress – a basis for ideas and discussion.

MORE WORDS OF WISDOM

As an organization embarks upon developing HR metrics, it will quickly become evident how important people are in achieving organizational success. The tendency might be to develop all sorts of measures to know everything we can about the performance of our key resources.

But beware – the success of a good HR metrics system is in developing the few measures that have the greatest impact and influence on organizational performance and sustainability.

It should be a continual process of thinking, developing, trying / testing, and improving. Remember the concept that, in great organizations, "amazing things get done by a group of average people." Despite the apparent "ease" of developing hard metrics about people, the better area to focus on would be measures that ensure sustainability of a culture that enables value to be created.

Aspects of resource / capital management			
1. Financial investment in human resources.			
Goal - understand cash flow investment in people (managing the "asset" that is invested in)			
A. Input (Availability of resource)	B. Process (Activity - use of resource)	C. Output (Result of process / activity)	D. Outcome* (value created by system)
• Cost per hire (past) • Recruitment costs (past) • HR budget % of total • HR budget / employee • Market value of enterprise including human capital	• Cost / hire (process) • Recruitment cost (process) • Cost of orientation / person • Investment in employees engaged in creating intellectual capital • Investment in employees engaged in relationship development • Investment in people to generate social capital • Investment in human capital development (team initiatives etc. to build collaboration) • Costs of absenteeism / sickness / unplanned leave • Overtime pay as % of base compensation	• Total workforce costs • Average pay / pay grade • Average pay / classification • Average pay / classification as % of market • Average benefit cost / person / grade • Total payroll as % of total costs • Total investment in current employees • Annual loss of investment in unplanned turnover • Ration of basic salary as % of total remuneration costs • Total training cost • Average training cost per FT employee • Average cost saving / employee suggestions •	• Cumulative investment in hiring workforce (hire plus orientation and basic training) • Cumulative investment in training leaders • Cumulative cost (net of decay and losses) of employee training • Value delivered / distributed to society • PTG pensions / retirement support • Fines / penalties linked to values, ethics, behavior • HR fines or penalties for non-compliance • HC-ROI • Reputation / brand value

Aspects of resource / capital management			
2A. Operational management of human resources			
Goal - effective management (use) of human resources			
A. Input (Availability of resource)	B. Process (Activity - use of resource)	C. Output (Result of process / activity)	D Outcome* (value created by system)
• Total number of employees	• Labor cost / unit output	• Lost time injury	• Client satisfaction (with human interactions)
• Number of FTE's	• # Additions to knowledge base / employee	• Number of occupational accidents	• Referrals by clients (based on personal experience)
• Contingent workforce	• # Accesses to knowledge base / employee	• Number of people killed during work	• Low premium rating for employee related insurance
• Independent contractors	• Enabling investment / employee (tools, equipment)	• EBIT / Revenue - turnover / profit per employee	• Low premium rating for workers compensation schemes
• Temporary / part time workforce by availability	• # Projects completed on time	• Human capital ROI	• Growth in enterprise market value
• Employees by position / qualification	• % Attendance at teamwork project meetings	• Direct : indirect ratio	• Growth in intellectual capital
• Male / female / other count	• # Of employees / % involved in cross-functional collaboration	• Absenteeism trend by cause	• Growth in relationship / social capital
• Full time / part time	• % / # Of employees engaged in creating intellectual capital	• Terminations for cause by reason	• Growth in manufactured capital
• Contract availability	• % / # Of employees engaged in relationship development	• Collaboration surveys	
• Retiree availability	• FTE time spent on enhancing human capital	• # Employee suggestions ideas submitted	
• Average years of service	• % / # Of new hires meeting performance goals	• # Employee suggestions implemented	
• Availability (% of each category)	• Average sick leave / employee	• # Employees of STD / LTD by cause	
• Tenure / experience / years in role		• # Of patents applied for / issued led by employee	
• Workforce bench strength			
• Workforce competency vs. plan			
• % Of or # Of critical positions			
• Succession readiness rates			

197

Human Capital Metrics

Aspects of resource / capital management 2A. Operational management of human resources *Goal - effective management (use) of human resources*			
A. Input (Availability of resource)	B. Process (Activity - use of resource)	C. Output (Result of process / activity)	D Outcome* (value created by system)
	• Volume / % E-mails in / out after work hours • % Hours worked on site / off site • % Hours worked "away from home" by category • # Of cross training / cross function opportunities •		

198

2B. Leadership of human resources
Goal - sustaining optimum climate for human resources

A. Input (Availability of resource)	B. Process (Activity - use of resource)	C. Output (Result of process / activity)	D Outcome* (value created by system)
• Diversity of leadership team • Span of control • Depth of leadership experience (years of service, ratings) • Level of developed leadership skills	• % Of leaders with formal mentors / coaches • % / $ of leader's time spent on personal development • New hire engagement rate (fitting in) • # Of incidents of harassment • # Complaints related to behavior • # Of disputes escalated • Absence rate / manager / department • Promotion rates by manager / department • Requests for transfer by manager / department • Performance rating distributions by manager • # Of coaching interventions • % Of employees by department at required competency level	• Number and type of grievances filed • Number and type of concluded disciplinary actions • Disputes referred to 3rd parties • # Of findings from 3rd party referrals • Exit / turnover rate by reason, manager, others • Voluntary turnover rate (ex. retirements) • Voluntary critical turnover rate • Involuntary turnover rate • Diversity of leadership team • Leadership trust • Turnover rate • % Managers below target performance level • % Of managers ready for promotion	• Turnover rate • Employee engagement • Composite culture rating • PTG "peaceful societies, justice" • PTG innovation • Local management % / # • Ranking as "preferred / good" employer • Organization reputation • Retention rate • Average length of service • Positive social media presence • Growth in human capital • Enhanced "change readiness"

A. Input (Availability of resource)	B. Process (Activity - use of resource)	C. Output (Result of process / activity)	D Outcome* (value created by system)
	• Loss rate of high performance / fast trackers	• # Managers ready for promotion as % of annual vacancy rate • Employee engagement score • Net promoter score • % Employees scoring managers over 90% • Trust rating • # or $ of employees aligned with purpose • % Rating of employees against stated values • Rating of managers to organizational values • % External trust / confidence in organization • # of employees who would recommend friends for vacant positions • Engagement rate in social activities • % Of employees engaged in sponsored initiatives	

2B. Leadership of human resources
Goal - sustaining optimum climate for human resources

2B. Leadership of human resources
Goal - sustaining optimum climate for human resources

A. Input (Availability of resource)	B. Process (Activity - use of resource)	C. Output (Result of process / activity)	D Outcome* (value created by system)
		<ul><li>% Of employees with satisfaction < 80%</li><li># Or trend of labor disputes</li><li># Or trend of disciplinary actions</li><li>Employee retention rate</li><li>Discrimination / harassment incidents (opened / proven)</li><li># Employees accessing EAP / EAR services</li><li>Results from 360° leadership assessments</li></ul>	

Aspects of resource / capital management 3 "Good Governance"			
Goal compliance, social responsibility, and optimum talent pool			
A. Input (Availability of resource)	B. Process (Activity - use of resource)	C. Output (Result of process / activity)	D Outcome* (value created by system)
• Diversity relative to age, diversity, gender, other • Workforce diversity by age • Workforce diversity by gender • Workforce diversity by disability • Workforce diversity other • Diversity of leadership team • Transition / future workforce capability assessment	• # Whistleblowing incidents • # Whistleblowing incidents investigated • # Of whistleblowing incidents showing proven problems. • Cycle time incident report to resolution	• Diversity relative to age, diversity, gender, other • % Of management position staffed by women • % Of management positions staffed by other minorities • %/ # Of positions earning with 10% of minimum wage • # Or % Of employees participating in sponsored health programs • New hires as % of workforce by age group • Pay gap across levels from "C" suite to lowest by level	• % Achievement of diversity goals • % Achievement of statutory diversity • PTG good jobs / decent work • PTG community development • PTG employee health • PTG gender equality • PTG sustainable business (strategic) • PTG reduce inequality • PTG continuity of employment / workforce • PTG Social capital

Aspects of resource / capital management			
4. HR management			
Goal - effective operation of HR processes			
A. Input (Availability of resource)	B. Process (Activity - use of resource)	C. Output (Result of process / activity)	D Outcome* (value created by system)
• # Of qualified candidates / position • Successor coverage rate • Internal mobility rate • % HR staffing positions filled	• Average length of time to fill vacant positions • Average length of time to fill critical positions • % Of vacant critical positions to all vacant positions • Recruitment rate • Applicants / recruitment rate • Applicant interest rate / % • Cycle time - requirement to fill • Cycle time, pay adjustments • Recruitment conversion rate (by stage) • Backlog of open positions • New hire satisfaction rate with orientation • % Of employees completing orientation within goal • % Of training programs delivered on time	• Percentage of employees who have completed training on compliance and ethics • % Of employees who participate in raining as % Of total employees • % Of position filled internally • % Of critical positions filled internally • Successor coverage rate • Succession effectiveness rate • Successor readiness rate % Within 1 -3 years • Successor readiness rate % Within 3 - 5 years • % Of positions filled internally • % Of critical positions filled internally • Average # of training hours / employee / year	• Employer of choice (at hiring / university, college etc.) • HR client satisfaction rate (as business partner) • PTG results of CHRO

Aspects of resource / capital management			
4. HR management			
Goal - effective operation of HR processes			
A. Input (Availability of resource)	B. Process (Activity - use of resource)	C. Output (Result of process / activity)	D Outcome* (value created by system)
	• Participant satisfaction with training (by program / by type) • Sponsor satisfaction with training approach / results • Hire program candidate diversity • Candidates reach rate by channel • Candidate conversion rate by channel • Job / position offer acceptance rate (also by source) • # / % of trainees delivering desired ROI post training • $ Of HR services available as self-service • Self-service portal user satisfaction rate	• Training hours / FTE vs. all FTE's • Training progress to plan • ears of experience by position • # Of employees completed orientation • # Employees completed mandatory training within timeframe • # Employees with current training plan • % Of key roles with identified successor ready • % Of key roles with no success identified • # Or % Of employees ready for retirement • Imminent retirees with successors in training • # Of contract positions terminating with 12 months • Quality of hire	

Aspects of resource / capital management			
4. HR management			
Goal - effective operation of HR processes			
A. Input (Availability of resource)	B. Process (Activity - use of resource)	C. Output (Result of process / activity)	D Outcome* (value created by system)
		• % Of new hires terminated after probation • % Of new hires resigning within 1 year • % Of HR processes meeting performance goals	

Choosing metrics for the model – summary
• Many existing metrics can be used to populate an "integrated model."
• The GRI metrics are some of the most mature for optional human capital reporting.
• Examples such as ISO 30414:2018 and the supporting technical specifications can be used to start the process.
• Gaps will be seen, especially in outcomes, where human capital needs to be linked to both organizational and "people" goals and objectives.
• Gaps also exist in the emerging "outcome" aspects of human capital especially the creation of other intangible capitals.
• Work will be needed to develop leadership, culture, and engagement metrics.
• Whole system composite indicators will also need to be developed.
• The metrics must be developed as an integral part of the planning process.
• The most mature aspect of HR metrics will probably be HR processes, but these will need to be supported by goals linked to key outcomes.
• Metrics will reflect resource availability (input), effectiveness and use of resources (activity), results of activities (outputs), and, finally, the achievement of organizational goals and objectives as high-level outcomes.

Choosing metrics for the model – checklist
• Start with what is available.
• Build using existing frameworks for ideas.
• Work backwards – think about outcomes desired, then processes and activities required to achieve these, and, finally, what resources are required.
• Success is not the number of metrics; in fact the opposite – aim for the critical few.
• Always ask "what do I need to know?" and "knowing this, what action I can take?"
• Take an "evolutionary" approach – try things, see what works and what is relevant, decide, then move on.

7 Measuring culture

The area of work climate, including employee engagement and corporate culture is rapidly developing. The brief discussion in this chapter complements the development of an effective culture outlined in my book *Corporate Culture*, which sets out the steps to understand, design, develop, measure, and sustain a desired culture within an organization. Culture is not a "quick fix" that many leaders want to adopt and embrace to "fix their culture challenges." To quote from *Corporate Culture*:

> *There is no right culture. No consulting firm can tell you how to solve your corporate culture "issues." It is like going to a marriage counsellor and asking them to "fix" your marriage. No two relationships are the same because no two people are the same. It is the same in business. Culture is unique to each organization. What makes it REALLY hard is that people are unique, fickle, and different. Many of their actions are driven as emotional responses, no matter how "committed" they are.*

The issue of developing an effective culture is also heavily dependent upon the quality and commitment of management and leadership at all levels. While it starts at the top, the message must be consistent and clear: *"this is the way we do business around here."* Leaders must be able to believe in their organization's direction, both its "purpose" (what we do) and "values" (how we behave when we do it). Only through this can they act with integrity and consistency and develop trust, which is an essential ingredient of a positive culture. Over many years of practical, hands-on experience with boards, leaders, all levels of supervision, union representatives and employees, the importance of the role of the leader was formulated into a series of approaches that are embedded in the book I co-wrote with Peter J. Smyth, *Reflective Leaders and High-Performance Organizations*. In this book we state:

> *The reality is that people, who work better within relational environments, are the ones who execute the tasks necessary to deliver outcomes and, through this, obtain financial results. The problem has been that no matter what new approaches, tools, and ideas are brought to bear on the execution of task, they often fall short of their potential because of their inability to engage the people.*

Organizational success depends upon getting results and staying ahead of the competition; historically, management has focused on the "tasks" necessary to achieve success. It is only now being realized that true leverage in task execution comes from the innovation and creativity of *engaged* people.

There is also a generally unknown impact of a poor culture. Because financial accounting and reporting do not tend to recognize waste attributable to less than optimum human performance, the potential improvements are never recognized. I demonstrate the financial impact of these invisible costs and lost opportunities in *The Cost of Poor Culture*, published in 2021. This book describes the impact of financial surprises, hidden operating costs, and the impact of lost opportunities that come from a lack of human engagement. Jeremy Eden and Terri Long, in *Low-Hanging Fruit*[31], also demonstrated the "untapped wealth" from buried costs that employees knew about but felt powerless to fix. Organizations such as Heinz, saved millions in operating costs just by changing the level of employee engagement.

The challenge of measuring culture is significant and for many organizations will evolve and mature over time. Effective approaches to

---

[31] Eden, Jeremy, and Long, Terri, *Low-Hanging Fruit: 77 Eye-Opening Ways to Improve Productivity and Profits*, 2014, Wiley.

culture metrics will evolve, the greater the understanding and awareness of the plans and actions needed to build and sustain a productive culture become. In this chapter, I suggest what the approaches will be at various stages in the journey; because the approach will evolve, the suggestions are shown by the stage of evolution, or phase in the development, shown in Table 7.1.

Table 7-1 The five stages of cultural awareness and development

#	Stage of Evolution	Explanation	Approach to cultural measurement
0	Natural	Belief that there is a culture but it has evolved rather than been planned	Generic questions in survey format
1	Awakening	Organization "Purpose" exists but behavior / culture not clearly defined	Generic questions in survey format supplemented by any "Purpose" items.
2	Early	"Values" statement has been created that defines "the way we do things around here"	Some generic but starting to add "validation" questions based on "values."
3	Evolving	"Values" embedded in all areas - hiring, orientation, leadership development, policies and procedures, feedback, compensation and all other aspects of operations.	Questions built on "Values" but including composite indicators of underlying satisfaction e.g. HR process performance.
4	Defined	Human behaviours are clearly aligned with operational goals and rank equally to "Purpose" at strategy level. People are a competitive advantage.	Multiple tools to assess holistic culture: surveys based on desired performance, leadership 360 assessments, client input, supplier input and others.

In the five stages of evolution, the concept of organizational culture starts from something that is talked about in the same way as "people are our greatest asset" but is not strategically embedded into the "DNA" of the way that the organization does business. From here, the "journey" moves to a defined and developed stage, where culture ranks equally to corporate purpose, and where the planning for processes, activities, tasks, and projects, ranks equally with ensuring and aligning the approach to being "human-centric" across all aspects of organizational activity.

7.1 Natural and Awakening stages of culture metrics

You cannot measure something unless there is a base to compare it against. While this sounds obvious, it is often not adopted in addressing metrics to evaluate culture. While organizational goals and objectives are established for what the organization *wants* to achieve, rarely do organizations set an equivalent level of importance on stating "how" it wants to achieve these things. Goals are established for growth, market share, profitability, quality, and other traditional performance criteria, and metrics are created and reported to assess how well this is being achieved. Only recently have goals for human "culture" activities started to appear.

As an example, in 2021, HC-IRC reviewed several studies in human capital reporting: One study showed 26% of respondents addressed culture (versus 60% on headcount and 54% on diversity and inclusion); another study showed 7% reporting on Principles and Values (with 53% on diversity and inclusion); yet another showed 44% discussed employee engagement, while another showed that 32% discussed engagement.

Also, one large employer, Deutsche Bank, published a human capital report for 2020, which contained a great many metrics, but also a statement about how the approach to human capital is viewed:

> The HR function provides the business with tools, frameworks and analyses that enable us to effectively manage our workforce. Effective workforce management plays a vital role in achieving transformational goals and includes supporting managers in performing their daily tasks, from recruitment to development and providing insights to senior management, which will in turn support strategy and planning activity and enable better informed decisions.

The bank follows this up with a KPI related to human capital that reads:

The Feedback Culture   By 2020: 68%

Survey was introduced in 2019 based on Deutsche Bank People Survey evidence showing the significant impact of regular and helpful conversations between managers and employees on commitment and enablement. The survey serves to assess the quality and frequency of top-down and bottom-up feedback and appreciation and aims to reinforce the right behavior and identify areas for further support.

This seems to represent both a traditional HR process thinking around human capital and a piecemeal approach to what is required to develop a strategic approach to culture. This is not strategically driven, system wide, human-centric culture development.

In stages 0 and 1 of cultural maturity (using ISO/TS 24178:2021 - Organizational Culture Metrics Cluster), the understanding of culture as a strategic issue has not yet developed. Many organizations may have implemented a "Statement of Purpose" (stage 1) but generally culture is not understood, planned, or aligned within the organization. Metrics at this stage will tend to rely on approaches such as:

- employee engagement surveys;
- employee satisfaction surveys;
- commitment surveys;
- outcome-based metrics, such as turnover; and
- tracking high-level outcomes such as retention.

There are good generic surveys that can be used and do create some level of valuable information. Additionally, organizations can choose to use tools such as generic leadership 360° assessments, which can provide some feedback in terms of leadership behavior that has an impact on the employees' engagement. Figure 7.1 shows a list of the sorts of generic survey questions that readers may be familiar with.

Figure 7.1 Basic engagement / satisfaction questions

		Strongly disagree	Disagree	Neutral	Agree	Strongly agree
1	Our organization has a clear purpose					
2	I am fairly compensated for my work					
3	I have clear direction for my work					
4	Workloads are usually reasonable					
5	Internal communications are effective					
6	I am treated fairly by the organization					
7	Employee suggestions are encouraged					
8	People cooperate in our organization					
9	People have the opportunity to develop					
10	Learning and development are encouraged					
11	I trust my supervisor					
12	Employees are recognized for good work					

There are standard online tools available, such as Survey Monkey, that provides a generic culture survey template. Survey templates are also available from organizations such as TalentLyft that have a combination of 14 questions using the Likert scale, most of which are about relationships, plus 10 open-ended questions that are about feelings related to the workplace. Other organizations, such as the Enterprise Engagement Alliance, use the ISO 10018:2020 *Guidance for People Engagement* as a foundation for the key principles. (This ISO document was developed by the group that developed the ISO 9001 Quality Management Standards.)

The problem with all of these approaches is that they do not directly link with *an organization's own goals and objectives*. Rather, they are generic and reflect "typical" aspects of factors that impact employee engagement and through that their base for an effective culture. Organizations that rely on this level of metrics will typically remain at the non-strategic levels of human engagement. Moving beyond this stage will require a strategic and structured approach to culture and, through this, to the metrics to be used.

7.2   Early and evolving stages of culture metrics

For culture metrics to move beyond the generic, an organization must define what it expects in terms of human behavior. While "Purpose" statements are sometimes assumed to fill this role, typically these are inadequate. Organizations that make a real, strategic commitment to people, will need to decide what this commitment "looks like." Examples can be cited such as the J&J Credo; this extract focuses on employees:

> *We are responsible to our employees who work with us throughout the world. We must provide an inclusive work environment where each person must be considered as an individual. We must respect their diversity and dignity and recognize their merit. They must have a sense of security, fulfillment, and purpose in their jobs. Compensation must be fair and adequate and working conditions clean, orderly, and safe. We must support the health and well-being of our employees and help them fulfill their family and other personal responsibilities. Employees must feel free to make suggestions and complaints. There must be equal opportunity for employment, development, and advancement for those qualified. We must provide highly capable leaders and their actions must be just and ethical.*

Another example is Adobe, which publishes information about the importance of its people. The following is an extract from the company website:

> *Culture is defined as "the ideas, customs, and social behavior of a particular people or society". Corporate culture centers around a set of values and beliefs in a workplace environment.*

> *Corporate culture is the backbone of any successful company. In 2016, computer software company, Adobe, was recognised in Fortune Magazine's '100 Best Companies to Work For', for the 16th time.*

Adobe then lists four specific core values that permeate their business, each having a broad potential application to "the way we do things around here":

- GENUINE. "We're sincere, trustworthy and reliable"
- EXCEPTIONAL. "We are committed to creating exceptional experiences that delight our employees and staff"
- INNOVATIVE. "We are highly creative and strive to connect new ideas with business realties"
- INVOLVED. "We are inclusive, open and actively engaged with our customers, partners, employees and the communities we serve"

Each of these values is explained in more depth at the Adobe website and makes interesting reading.

Handelsbanken, a long-established Swedish financial services company, makes no secret of its focus on business with the following statement:

> *Our goal*
> *Handelsbanken's goal is to have better profitability than the average of peer competitors in its home markets.*
>
> *This goal is mainly to be achieved by the Bank having more satisfied customers and lower costs than its competitors.*

However, it then lays out specific "modes of operations" that create the foundation of "how" it will achieve this goal, many of which have a direct relationship to behavior in the "way we do things around here." The following seven points are their key ways of working:

- *Trust-based management*
- *A decentralised organisation*
- *Customer first – not products*
- *Up close and personal*
- *A responsible role in society*

- *A long-term perspective*
- *Profit-sharing for all employees*

Handelsbanken has won major awards for its performance and has not been hit by many of the scandals that have impacted the financial services industry over the last 20 years.

Why are these examples important? Because unless an organization can state clearly, as goals and objectives, what it expects in terms of the culture, then it is almost impossible to create effective metrics to measure it. In all these examples, the company can now do four things:

1. Convert intent into operational reality by asking: How do we make this happen in terms of policies, practices, and procedures?
2. Align operating practices to ensure they support the stated requirements of behavior.
3. Ensure that key "people" activities, such as recruitment, orientation, training, leadership development, and employee performance management, all reflect and support "the way we do things."
4. Create a system of metrics that assess whether the expected "ways of doing things" are in fact what is being experienced by employees and other stakeholders.

The steps of converting intent into reality is covered in *Corporate Culture* which explains how an organization asks itself: What would be happening if we were true to this statement? and What would we *not* be doing if we were true to this statement? The answers to these questions then drive policies and procedures, as well as supervisory development, hiring, and other activities. Once this happens, metrics can be developed that ask: Are we doing these things?

As an example, based on the Adobe core values, the *genuine* aspect could be validated by questions (created as my example), such as:

		Strongly disagree	Disagree	Neutral	Agree	Strongly agree
1	People are attentive to my ideas					
2	My supervisor is not judgemental					
3	People are open and share ideas					
4	People are treated with respect					
5	The workplace is based on trust					
6	People are "down to earth" and honest					
7	People act with integrity					

Figure 7.2 Examples of questions that link values with actual results

Using this approach, an organization can create clear expectations of behavior; build operating processes, activities, and tasks that reflect these; select, train, and develop both employees and leaders using these expectations; and, finally, ask questions that validate whether or not expectations are being met.

This may be seen as too detailed or complex. It is not short-term nor is it simple; nor will it be perfect. But unless expectations are stated, there is no assurance that actual behavior will be demonstrated. People are unique in their backgrounds, personalities, and beliefs and an organizational culture can be strengthened by this. However, if there is not a defined statement of expectations (goals), then there will be no way to measure progress. The importance of this approach is that it treats the behavior aspects of business in exactly the same way as the tasks required to achieve the goals and objectives. In Chapter 5, the strategic importance of metrics was illustrated by using the PDCA model (Plan, Do, Check and Act). This can be applied again here.

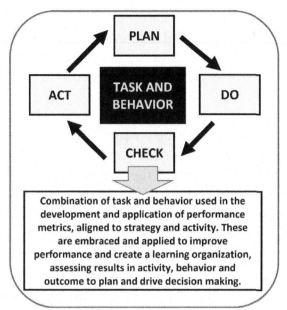

Figure 7.3 Building human capital metrics as part of the PDCA model

As can be seen in Figure 7.3, the whole management approach combines both task and behavior – what is to be done and expectations around how it is to be accomplished.

The "Do" segment is where the alignment is important, as it establishes behavioral expectations in terms of work environment – both supervisory behavior and the way in which processes operate. This process element is a key aspect of "doing what you say you do." This is often a problem in organizations and an aspect that reduces employee commitment and depletes a positive culture.

7.3   From Evolving to Defined stages of culture metrics

This final stage of the evolution of culture reflects metrics that validate the statements of expectations together with other metrics that demonstrate an element of factors contributing to culture. The first aspect is based on people's opinions about the culture – what they see as opposed to what has been communicated as expectations. (Hence the importance of the "Values" statements or equivalent and the translation of this into "the way we work.") The second aspect will be to combine these personal opinions with other more objective and fact-based aspects of human capital activities.

One of the main examples of this will be the combined effectiveness of the human resources processes – a composite measure of process performance. There might also be the results of a separate (or independent) salary survey that indicates the impact of compensation. Figure 7.4 shows an example about how an "enterprise" culture metric might be constructed.

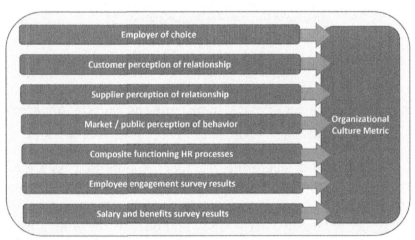

Figure 7.4 Measuring culture as a composite

Each line item might be a single metric, or it could be a combination of metrics that have then been weighted. Looking at each aspect of what makes up the total "human experience:"

- Employer of choice (which may also be a standalone human capital goal), could be a single question or feedback from multiple sources.
- Customer perception: feedback from customers and clients relative to the human interaction experienced in dealings with the organization, e.g., support, complaints, problems. This could also include metrics related to call-centre satisfaction.
- Supplier perception: similar to customer perception, but might include multiple areas of interaction, e.g., purchasing, design, support, administration, shipping.
- Market / public perception: public feedback relative to human interactions; in particular, aspects of brand and reputation feedback (sourced from metrics around sustaining the value of the brand relative to human behavior). It might also include community feedback related to monitoring the human aspects of relationships within the community; or feedback from other third parties such as regulatory feedback.
- Composite functioning of HR processes: an indicator showing the overall performance of HR processes (that should typically be functioning at a high performance level to support employee engagement and thus contribute to a positive culture).
- Employee engagement: direct input from surveys or assessment provided by employees using the questions discussed above, based on the organization's stated expectations.
- Salary surveys: typically segregated from satisfaction or engagement surveys, these would contribute an aspect of positive or negative culture.

As can be seen, the development of metrics relative to culture is not a simple task of deciding which questions to ask and administering a survey; while this aspect forms an essential element of organizational culture, there is a complex foundation that must exist for a desired culture to be developed, deployed, implemented, measured, sustained, and improved. *This is why human capital has a value to an organization and why the investment made to build a culture forms part of the market value of any successful organization.*

Culture summary
• Culture is an organization-level, strategy driven issue.
• Most organizations start measuring culture through focusing on generic employee satisfaction-style metrics.
• Effective culture metrics can only be developed when the organization establishes expectations for "behavior."
• These expectations are usually referred to as "values."
• Once defined, organizations must align their operating infrastructure with the desired behavior (hiring, orientation, training / development, performance review, leadership development).
• Once expectations have been defined, metrics can be developed that ask questions to assess the effectiveness of deployment.
• Culture metrics will evolve as the strategic approach to culture becomes embedded in the organization.
• Major culture metrics will become high-level composite measures that assess a broad base of feedback on behavior.

Culture checklist
• Is there a "rapid feedback" system for determining employee satisfaction (as a base metric approach)?
• Has the organization defined and developed what it means by culture in a set of "values-based" expectations?
• Has the organization determined what operational reality would look like if behavior aligned with expectations?
• Have these expectations been converted and aligned with operating approaches, policies, procedures, and methodology?
• Have questions been developed that directly link back to and validate stated expectations (goals) that can be measured against?
• Have multiple aspects of culture been considered and metrics developed to create a composite organizational culture metric?

8 The changing expectations of society

Organizations have always been part of society, but their role and position are constantly changing as is the public's perception of their behavior as part of that society. Sometimes, to understand the ideas and proposals of an author, it is useful to look behind the "thinking" and see some of the context that drives their opinion and desire for change. For this purpose, I share some of my ideas (see Figure 8.1).

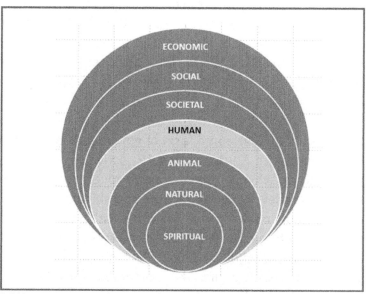

Figure 8-1 Humans create and manage the social systems we live within

As people – human beings – we live within a system. Some of the system we created but other, foundational pieces we did not.

Spiritual, natural, and animal aspects are not directly of our making (although some aspects such as spiritual are open to debate). We, as people are here. Over the years, we have evolved both individually and collectively. In one way or another, we are all members of a society which for many of us provided our underlying social norms and practices. We collectively developed these and, as a society, largely adhere to them. In some cases, we have developed rules that specifically define expected behaviour; in other cases, we rely on "expected behaviour." (Many will recognize this as a foundation of the discussion on ethics.)

Within these societies, we have evolved economic systems which we have organized in a way that meets our needs for basic requirements (food, water), eventually extending beyond needs to "wants." (Many will also recognize the underlying development of this hierarchy of needs from the work of Maslow.) Typically, these economic systems were aligned with the society within which we lived and reflected the social expectations within that society. Thus, our economic systems and the rules, norms, and practices through which they were created and under which they operate are of our own (human) creation. If we want to change them, we can do so.

Each society tends to have some form of governance that establishes the rules under which its "human-created" activities, such as business, operate. Therefore, when problems occur, governments respond. Thus, when an increasing level of corporate accountability problems occured in the USA, that society passed laws such as the Sarbanes–Oxley Act of 2002. Governments also bring in regulatory frameworks to guide and monitor organizations – such as regulations covering health and safety and financial conduct. As was discussed earlier, this is where significant change has been occurring in recent decades.

- The global mobility of people has started to separate the linkage between an individual's "home" society and the society where they live and work.
- Economic activity has moved from an "in society" framework to a global framework, so that the conduct of business no longer reflects that of its home society alone.
- As these changes in economic activity have taken place, most regulation remains at the "local" societal level and, therefore, is often seen as inconsistent.
- The flow of capital and the flow of information (as well as products and services) have also become global, resulting in competitive advantage becoming a global challenge.

"Business in society" might look like Figure 8.2, where the grey box with dotted lines reflects where business sits.

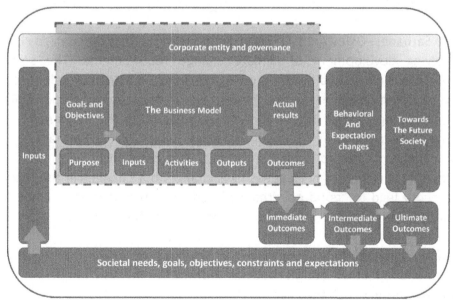

Figure 8-2 Business models are a "construct" within society

Society is the "big picture", but business is one of many entities within society whose activities impact a broad range of stakeholders. While business activity is based on societal needs and opportunity, and uses these as inputs, one may believe that "the job is done" when the business model delivers the desired outcomes. But, from a societal perspective, business outcomes are only considered "immediate outcomes." These results from business activity then permeate back into society and have an impact. People's lives change not only from what products and services business delivers but also from how it behaves while doing this. These are bigger "intermediate outcomes." When these outcomes demonstrate undesired impact to society, especially when they seem to be heading in a direction that may not be desired, two things may happen:

1. Legislation may be enacted to create further demands or constraints on the conduct of business, or
2. Public attitudes will change and will eventually impact business planning.

The Sarbanes–Oxley Act (SOX) is an example of the first outcome, as is the evolving development of climate change requirements. The second outcome is illustrated by the growing challenge in attracting talent to an organization based on the public's perception of corporate responsibility. The challenge is that organizations *must* respond to the items in #1, but have the option of changing strategy based on governance and management decision making in #2. Noncompliance with the first outcome is increasingly illegal as laws change, but changes in the second category lead to "good governance," reflecting the need to balance the changing importance of stakeholders other than shareholders.

These changes that businesses are "forced" to make, are having a profound effect on people both as individuals and as members of the society within which they live.

Organizations will seek to optimize all "costs of capital" to meet global competition. This results in:

- raising financial capital in the lowest-cost environments;
- employing human capital in the lowest-cost environments;
- building global relationships with least-cost suppliers;
- building sales / distribution relationships wherever possible;
- seeking the lowest regulatory / regulatory-cost environments; and
- generating profits (financial capital) in the lowest tax regime environments.

These changes are increasingly seen as concerns about the way organizations operate – yet they are not illegal. However, they reflect the reality of global competition. Various international bodies have become increasingly involved in collaborating and influencing governments towards "normalizing" regulations. Nations (societies) are also collaborating to try and align approaches to the environment within which businesses operate. A few examples might include:

- G7 group of nations.
- G20 Group of nations.
- Conduct and operational agreements in free trade agreements.
- United Nations Social Development goals (SDGs).
- Work of various UN agencies.
- Work of the OECD (Organization for Economic Cooperation and Development).
- Trade blocs and multi-national communities, such as the EU.
- World Business Council on Sustainable Development (WBCSD).
- World Economic Forum.

These activities all take place in a world where governments are primarily elected by their citizens and, therefore, reflect local needs, typically before bowing to international pressures. Businesses face a challenge in navigating these changes, driving a course that balances pressure from customers and society in terms of their "license to operate" and being able to meet global competition and survive.

A key stakeholder in these challenges is the financial investor. As money flows across and between borders, investors are increasingly aware of risk related to certain aspects of business conduct that represent the value and sustainability of their investment. The growing awareness related to the environment and climate change has become a core issue, with investors demanding (as far as possible) certain actions by those they invest in, to recognize the challenge and change their methods of operation accordingly.

Certain other "conduct" issues have also become recognized and are subject to evaluation by investors. One key example is the movement of garment manufacturers from the "developed" world to less developed economies and the subsequent revelations of problems such as unsafe working conditions, child labour, worker exploitation, and others. These issues resulted in a voluntary global standard, SA 8000 (Social Accountability), which has since been followed by ISO 26000 on Corporate Social Responsibility.

Such issues have become important to investors because they have seen a growing risk to their investment value – not only in terms of short-term damage but also related to the sustainability of the business model of their investment.

The drive for greater transparency in corporate reporting and accountability – and within this human capital reporting – falls within this framework of evolution. Regulators are responding to public concern over "license to operate" but also to growing concern from investors about the integrity and value of their investment.

Building the business case to clearly identify the linkage between human capital on the one hand and the sustainability and continuity of the business and the risk to investors on the other will continue to be a critical aspect of the development of enhanced human capital metrics. Table 8.1 suggest some linkages.

Table 8-1 Metrics within a societal context

DRIVER	DESCRIPTION OF SPAN OF METRICS
Legislated	Metrics imposed by legislation to demonstrate compliance
Reputational	Metrics developed that clearly demonstrate link between human capital and sustaining brand value or reputation
Growth	Metrics developed that clearly link market focused value creation with the existence, nurturing and innovation that drives growth and **revenue**
Value	Metrics developed that demonstrate a clear linkage between the market value of an organization and the **quality** of its workforce and its operations
Risk	Metrics that clearly demonstrate the risk to an organizations continuity and the well being of the workforce
Operational	Metrics that clearly demonstrate a linkage between investments in human capital and the return on this in terms of **output, cost** and productivity

One approach that might be important is to better understand the linkage between an organization's brand and reputation and its human capital. As was discussed earlier, a significant element of the unexplained value of an organization is the amount attributed to its financial brand value. Many of the aspects of investing in human capital are focused on carrying out activities and tasks that support and enhance brand value.

The development of human capital metrics is being seen as a welcome step by many in the human resources community; however, to embed the need for such metrics they must go beyond "nice to have" and meet one or more of the suggested criteria in Table 8.1. This requires a constant examination of the link between the business goals and objectives, an effective analysis of the gap between current state and desired state, and, where relevant, a human capital-driven strategy, through which the investment in and nurturing of human capital is seen as a priority.

Well-run organizations that meet societal needs through the creation of needed products and services, and by creating employment and generating broad-based benefits are important. The growth in well-being and the lifting of poverty in many areas can be shown to be a result of the growth of business. However, as society evolves, the expectations of the public will change. This is the global context within which integrated reporting and broad-based performance and accountability metrics are developing.

9   Total-system performance

What if there were a new, human-centric, whole-system metric? The evolution of corporate performance reporting has been heavily weighted towards financial capital. Within this a single metric has evolved that combines everything that an organization does. This metric is called "profit." Everything is converted to financial value; if there is more financial capital at the end of the period than at the beginning, the "system" is deemed to have worked effectively. The assumption is that the more profit an organization makes, the more effectively it is being managed. We have seen that this assumption is no longer accurate.

The following section is extracted from my book, *The Cost of Poor Culture*; it discusses the evolving problems that have started to occur related to organizational culture – the "behavior that people exhibit." It focuses on the issue of financial surprises.

9.1   Extract from *The Cost of Poor Culture*

Reporting problems, disclosure issues, and ethical scandals, have demonstrated that beneath apparent financial success other problems are lurking undetected. These are unrecognized risks that any approach to human capital metrics should help disclose. The financial impact of poor culture falls into one of three impacts – financial surprises, buried operating costs and hidden or lost opportunities leading to competitive problems.

Financial surprises involve actions that take place, that were unexpected and will typically have a negative financial impact on the organization.

These events and surprises occur in widely held, publicly traded organizations, in which the system of governance, including audits and reporting, should protect against illegal or unethical actions, or other non-financial losses or impacts. One might assume, in these cases, that the events came as a surprise to those responsible. They may have occurred with board knowledge of the risk, or by management acting on its own authority or by individuals or small groups acting alone.

Financial surprises can be looked at in two groups – those caused by individual action, and those caused by the organization as a whole. Individual actions leading to surprises would include those of Nick Leeson at Barings Bank in 1995, which resulted in the bank's collapse.

This was a classic case where inattention to culture increased the risk of financial problems; if people are left to their own "devices" with little or no guidance (and poor oversight / governance) then results will be unpredictable! There is a great quote on the University of Essex website that provides a history of scandals and frauds[32] :

> **"Bankers who hire money hungry geniuses should not always express surprise and amazement when some of them turn around with brilliant, creative, and illegal means of making money."**
>
> *The quotation is from a speech by the financial thriller writer Linda Davies, on "The Psychology of Risk, Speculation and Fraud", at a conference on EMU in Amsterdam.*

Figure 9-1 Risk and hungry bankers

It appears that, even before he arrived in Singapore, the risk existed; Nick Leeson was "less than honest[33]" when applying for his broker's license.

---

[32] https://projects.exeter.ac.uk/RDavies/arian/scandals/classic.html

[33] Scott, Hal S., 2006. *International Finance: Transactions, Policy, and Regulation.* Foundation Press.

There have been several other cases of rogue traders acting alone in the financial services industry. These might be considered "control" surprises, but what about the larger corporate surprises? In their desire to build innovative, creative financial solutions and activities the human capital system failed in its ability to provide adequate controls.

Looking at the "big picture," publicly available data reveal that, in the USA, penalties and fines imposed on organizations over the last twenty years have exceeded $490 billion; that is $490 billion charged for anything from safety violations to illegal acts, lack of protection of privacy, fraud, and many others. Note how many of these issues relate to the action of human capital.

It would be unfair to generalize about these unplanned charges – in fact, some may be the result of management decisions to accept certain levels of risk, so that when an unplanned incident occurs, paying the fine is part of the cost of doing business. The table below lists the top six in total penalties imposed:

Parent organization	Cumulative cost in $ billions
Bank of America	$82.764
JPMorgan Chase	$35.819
BP	$29.197
Citigroup	$25.454
Volkswagen	$23.780
Wells Fargo	$21.359

Figure 9-2 Examples of financial surprises – maybe linked to culture?

Probably one of the most obvious costs relative to poor culture is demonstrated by the financial meltdown between 2008 and 2010, which caused the near collapse of the financial services industry; it can be seen from the table above that banks and other financial services organizations suffered heavily from fines imposed in the years following these problems. But this was not the only problem.

Wells Fargo arrived at a $3 billion settlement in 2020[34] for offences that apparently occurred between 2002 and 2016 related to the opening of fraudulent accounts. This was a widely publicized event and had a significant impact on both the firm's reputation, value and, of course, finances! It can be concluded that the internal direction given by leaders to "open new accounts" and the expectations of staff (as well as financial compensation) were not aligned. This example may well have been a situation caused by people doing what they thought to be acceptable – again a cultural issue. They were, after all opening these accounts based on "direction" imposed by quotas and managed by those in leadership positions. Was such illegal and unethical conduct acceptable to meet quotas or was it just part of "the way we do things around here?"

Another example is Volkswagen; many will remember this scandal, often referred to as Dieselgate, in which fuel consumption / mileage claims were generated incorrectly. Could it be that, in this situation, the engineers working in the company thought they were doing the right thing and finding a way to meet the fuel consumption requirements? Did senior leadership even know about it? Why didn't anybody blow the whistle? What type of culture allowed this to be done?

While one can concentrate on the large numbers that hit the headlines, this does not tell the whole story. The top six organizations in the list of US fines and penalties, account for almost 40% of the total $490 billion, yet using the data available from Violation Tracker[35], it can also be seen that there were over 480,000 individual fines and violations.

---

[34] See NY Times and other reports
[35] See https://violationtracker.goodjobsfirst.org/parent-totals

Looking at five specific cases the story may be different. For Volkswagen, three of the offences (related to Dieselgate) account for over 90% of their total fines and penalties; could this suggest that the overall governance is good but that the fuel economy lapse was more of a one-off problem? In the cases of Wells Fargo and Bank of America, the average fines are extremely high, and the number of offences is almost the same, but the average cost is lower. Does this suggest that Wells Fargo is relatively better than Bank of America?

Parent organization	Cumulative cost in $ billions	# of items	Average fine or penalty
Bank of America	$82.764	219	$377.9M
Volkswagen	$23.780	57	$424.6M
Wells Fargo	$21.359	182	$117.4M
Canadian National Railways (CNR)	$0.014	559	$25,856
Union Pacific	$0.183	3,298	$55,486

Figure 9-3 Are fines and penalties random or systemic?

Looking at a totally different industry, we can see that the railroads seem to have much lower average fines, although, upon investigation, it seems that almost all the events are safety-related, and the fines are much smaller. Does this tell us anything about either CNR or Union Pacific? Are these maybe the acceptable costs of doing business? However, might this contravene a safety-based culture, which is what both railroad companies are very conscious of? The fact is that ALL these events were unplanned, or if planned then clearly illegal and/or unethical. Were they sanctioned?

To these costs, particularly in financial services, can be added the prior societal impact of bailouts from various national governments; in the USA alone, the official number was about $700 billion, but broader-based *assessments[36] put the numbers much higher, with $4.6 trillion paid out and a total commitment that can be up to $16.8 trillion. There would also be societal costs associated with areas such as health and safety impacts.*

While it is a smaller amount, GM was fined $1 million by the Securities and Exchange Commission (SEC) over ignition switch problems that apparently killed at least 124 people (small price to pay!) on top of at least $595 million that the company paid out to victims[37]. The CEOs' responses to these fines are interesting: GM's CEO, Mary Barra, told the House Energy and Commerce Subcommittees she was aiming "...to correct a culture that has displayed a pattern of incompetence and neglect." This links the problem right back to behavior, but doesn't it seem to leave hanging the role of leadership? Why did people act in a way that was either unethical or illegal?

The key point in the sorts of prosecutions detailed above might be less the impact of the fines and penalties and more the damage that the conduct had on "social capital," that is, the relationships with employees and the sort of conduct they saw as acceptable. In many cases, the levels of fines amounted to a small proportion of income. (A detailed analysis was not performed because the dates of the various events, the delays and challenges of prosecution and the date the penalties were decided are almost impossible to reconcile to the income in the year or years that the events took place. Additionally, several organizations went through mergers and acquisitions during the period, especially in the financial services.)

As can be seen from these examples, the costs associated with surprises can be significant, and have both financial and reputational impacts; at

---

[36] "The Big Bank Bailout," *Forbes Magazine*, July 2014 (Mike Collins). https://www.forbes.com/sites/mikecollins/2015/07/14/the-big-bank-bailout/#31bda9aa2d83
[37] *USA Today* http://www.usatoday.com/story/money/cars/2017/01/18/general-motors-securities-and-exchange-commission-sec-ignition-switch/96717570/

worst, they can lead to the collapse of a whole sector, such as the financial meltdown in 2008–2010. Financial reporting informed investors about these issues after the fact. Could investors have been better prepared for these risks?

If one looks at the financial services industry, not every bank participated in the actions that led to the collapse. What was the difference? Were the other banks more prudent? Was their culture more risk averse? Did every employee understand where the line was drawn, beyond which they could not go in decision making?

If we drill down further, is it possible to say that the less risky banks' approach to hiring and compensation was more driven by hiring people with the "right values" and compensating employees and executives in a way that did not encourage undesired behavior? Was there an orientation program and was it effective? Was the whistle-blower program more effective? Was there a greater level of trust, communication, collaboration, and cooperation within the bank? How are leaders selected, developed, managed, and compensated? These are all features of the maturity and culture with which the organization is managed. If investors don't have visibility into their organization's maturity, they have little protection against surprises that reduce earnings and deplete value and, at worst, void their investment completely.

A growing category of surprises is the increase in Impairment losses that are being incurred by corporations; these happen after a merger or acquisition where the buyer pays more for the acquired organization than its book (accounting) value. In effect, the cost of buying the business as a system capable of earning an income stream is justified at this higher market price, and this "premium over book price" appears as an (intangible) asset on the buyer's financial records, recorded as "goodwill."

This is obviously a cost incurred by the shareholders of the buying organization that is funded from either diluting the value of their own shares or taking on more debt. When management and/or the auditors determine that this asset (goodwill) is worth less than is shown in the records, it is considered to have been "impaired" and the amount must be taken as a financial loss. Why?

"Over the last five years, there have been a total of 1,556 events in which goodwill has been considered impaired and written off (or written down) by publicly-traded companies incorporated in the United States." The total cost of this has been $270.4 billion[38].

While there are many issues and challenges behind these numbers, a key issue is that part of what the buyer was willing to pay for was "the system" that included the culture which gave the acquisition some of its market value. Could one believe that this was a surprise?

****

The main point from this extract, used to demonstrate the financial impact of these "human behaviours," is that financial reporting and audits suggested everything was OK. They revealed almost nothing about the underlying activities and risks that were playing out to earn income. There's no question, business requires risks to be taken – but were these "controlled risks" or failures of "the system" to carry out the conversion of inputs to outputs and outcomes in the desired context? Certainly, before many of these events happened, profits were being earned. All appeared good. But there was an unknown and unreported risk.

The game of business has changed and all stakeholders, including investors, need greater assurances that there will be no surprises. *Could there then be a more effective "full-system" indicator than profit?* One that embraces the complete business model including non-financial resources

---

[38] https://www.duffandphelps.com/insights/publications/goodwill-impairment/2020-us-goodwill-impairment-study

that more accurately assesses the health and quality of the system? Could something like this be included as a high-level composite metric within the human capital family? The answer is yes; while there are numerous approaches, the metric developed by the UK-based Maturity Institute – described in the next section – has some appeal. It is based on researched factors within the business model and has also been evaluated and correlated to enhanced organizational performance and sustainability. It is also based on a rating system that might be familiar to those, traditionally assessing financial risk.

9.2   An approach to a composite "health" metric

The UK-based Maturity Institute (MI) was established in 2012 as a new, multi-disciplinary, professional development institution, to help all enterprises address their changing, global ESG responsibilities. MI's purpose is to maximise the creation of Total Stakeholder Value (TSV), which incorporates both company performance and societal value. It integrates all management disciplines into a single, coherent, organizational system under a common purpose of TSV.

Ten pillars form the foundation for the MI's framework. These integrated values and principles explain the value–risk connections between all the people in the organization and those linked to it. When measured holistically, they present a complete picture of organizational maturity, where human governance and human capital management are fully integrated with, and motivated by, a whole system underpinned by the common pursuit of TSV. The 10 pillars form the basis from which to allow comparative assessment and rating of an organization's ability to create value and manage risk from human capital. The assessment approach and rating system is referred to as OMINDEX® (Organizational Maturity Index). The OMINDEX® diagnostic is increasingly used by investors as a key ESG measure, and by corporates as a Total Value Management system.

OMINDEX® is a comparative, company-focused performance rating system, developed and licensed by the Maturity Institute. The methodology that produces the comparative ratings assesses how companies create value relative to their effective capacity. Two unique ingredients in this rating system are:

- a clinical focus on the returns achieved, and achievable, from human capital, leadership practice, and management systems; and
- an ability to measure the delivery of value to all stakeholders – called Total Stakeholder Value.

This is not just a radically different, corporate performance measurement system, it provides a detailed diagnostic to identify areas for significant value improvements and risk reduction. It does so by asking 32 high-level, causal, qualitative questions about core ESG, human capital, and intangible systems, each with a subset of questions that provide objective evidence of additional value creation. Figure 9.4 shows an extract of these questions.

	TOPIC	QUESTION
1	Corporate Purpose	Does the organization have a clearly stated Purpose? Does the Purpose of societal value have clear primacy in the organization?
6	Trust	To what extent are the leadership and management team trusted by the customers, employees, and other key stakeholders?
7	Values	Have at least three core values been expressed by the organization?
13	Strategic cohesion	To what extent do leadership, management and staff understand and work cooperatively towards a coherent set of strategic goals?
14	Culture	What evidence is there that the Board recognizes and understands the importance of organizational culture and is it being monitored effectively?

Figure 9-4 OMINDEX questions related to culture

While the questions are publicly available, the use and application of the system and its approach to weighting and scoring are subject to completing the required training as an assessor. This means that assessments carried out are conducted on a consistent baseline and verification approach. The sample shown provides an insight into the type of items covered (with the relevant question number). The additional sample questions in Figure 9.5 also show that the assessment is broad-based, covering both the Purpose (that drives activities, tasks, and processes) and Values (and other items related to culture).

	TOPIC	QUESTION
15	System	To what extent does the organization operate as a coherent and cohesive whole system?
23	Value and human capital	To what extent are business improvement based on linking human capital to the variables of OCRQE? (Output, Cost, Revenue etc.)?
24	Return on human capital	Has the organization adopted a discipline of linking human capital directly to financial returns by completing ROI calculations?
32	Authenticity	What size is the gap between the organization's statements, external communications and claims of success relative to the reality found in the evidence?

Figure 9-5 Additional OMINDEX questions related to culture

Note the last question, in particular – one that frequently results in failure in building an effective culture; in other words: Does the organization deliver on what it says?

The responses to all these questions are based on publicly available information; this is a similar approach to that used by many investment advisors, who now use "alternative data" which "sweep" publicly available – and sometimes private – sources to obtain information on organizational activity. With the internet, analysts using OMINDEX® can obtain a large amount of information about an organization's behaviour in areas over and above traditional financial data. Several organizations which have worked with the OMINDEX® have been able to directly interview organizations and obtain inside information that further enhances the quality of their data.

Once all the data gathering has been completed and rated, a standard weighting system is applied based on Maturity Institute research and experience, and this produces a final "score" for the organization. This score provides a rating using the same scale as the S&P credit ratings, and should be familiar to many. The results can then be plotted on a scale, as shown in Figure 9.6.

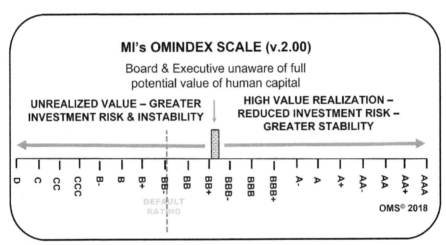

Figure 9-6 The OMINDEX® rating scale for people-centric maturity

The highest rating score – AAA – represents the MI view of an effective, full-system approach to human capital, which from an S&P risk standpoint would reflect the lowest risk. At the other end of the scale, D reflects "no explicit management method for people." S&P would see this as an organization in default with no creditworthiness.

The midpoint between BBB− and BB+ (see Figure 9.6) reflects the position that MI's research suggests is the point where the Board and Executive are unaware of the full potential of human capital. In other words, this is the point where "they don't know what they don't know" because there is nothing telling them. Whilst poor performance might be evident from the financial reports, this might be interpreted as the need for cost cutting rather than looking for constraints in the human system. The topics discussed in *The Cost of Poor Culture* present an example of the information that needs to be available to start developing this awareness. Existing human capital metrics do very little to enlighten users about the hidden impact of culture and engagement.

The default rating of BB− reflects where most organizations that have been evaluated would tend to score. Readers may be familiar with the hidden impact of poor process management, which faced a similar problem in that only by understanding the current levels of (often hidden) failure did organizations start to realize the potential. Figure 9.7 presents a familiar chart that illustrates this point.

SIGMA level	Defects per million (transaction, units)	Rating	Financial impact
2	308,537	Non-competitive	Unknown
3	66,807		25 – 40% of sales
4	6,210	Industry average	15 – 25% of sales
5	233		5 – 15% of sales
6	3.4	World class	< 1% of sales

Figure 9-7 The original process-based 6 Sigma levels

What if the frequency of events were not process "errors" but "human errors of judgement" or unplanned activities or behaviors? The term SIGMA is a statistical measure of variation from which the well-known term "6 Sigma" comes from, as being the aspirational ambition for performance of key business processes.

The important observation is that most organizations typically operate at about 4 Sigma, which represented 6,201 defects per million operations. More importantly, when it was realized what the underlying hidden impact of this level of failure was financially (equivalent to 15% or more of sales), it quickly became important. In the early years of adopting this concept of improved process management, organizations saw significant benefits; GE, for example, reported savings that exceeded $3–4 billion in one of the first years of adopting the concept. The buried potential that was yesterday's process failure costs is probably today's human failure costs, but these remain buried.

A maturity rating (as shown in Figure 9.8) will provide a single integrated metric about how the whole organization is approaching human capital, right from its inclusion and centrality at the strategic planning and development stage, through to effective deployment, including the use of metrics and the actions taken as a result of the metrics' feedback. In short, this deals with culture – the way the organization does things relative to its human capital.

The question set used has been developed around research (and has been validated). It is comprehensive in this it includes policy, procedures, results and most importantly the possibility of a gap between the words that are said about organizational values relative to being people centric and the reality that people see on a daily basis. Trained assessors who use the checklist are encouraged to both question people within the organization directly, as well as conduct independent third party research. The practise mirrors the developing approach of investment advisors who use tools like "web crawlers" to search out references about the organziation.

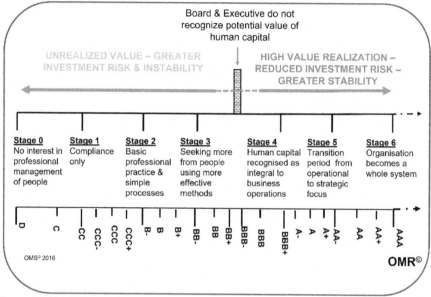

Figure 9-8 The OMINDEX® rating showing stages of maturity

These maturity ratings can then be transformed into "stages of maturity" providing some level of recognition of the level of centrality of human capital. The reality appears to be, from the assessments already completed, that most organizations, operating as discussed at BB−, are at the very early stages of appreciation of the strategic importance of human capital.

Some may be offended and disagree with this. Existing "mature" approaches to human resources management tend to be seen as focusing on management of human resources "policies, processes and activities", but this is the tip of the "opportunity iceberg." While more professionalism and structure, including the development of human capital metrics, supported by analytics, is important, it is does *not* reflect a centrality of human capital at the <u>strategic</u> level.

While organizations are starting to be aware of culture and employee engagement, many have no structured or managed approach to understanding the issue or embedding human capital in the same way that financial capital is managed. *If* organizations, especially at the governance and executive levels, begin to understand this "gap" and the risk it presents, then a more structured and holistic approach might start to develop (see Figure 9.9). If the frequency of "errors in judgment" reflected in the 6 Sigma "normal distribution" holds true (which it should), then what is the behavioral risk?

SIGMA level	Errors in judgement per million actions / decisions	Sigma "competitive" Rating	Potential risk of unplanned or unexpected behavior leading to loss
2	308,537	Non-competitive	High risk
3	66,807		Medium to high risk
4	6,210	Industry average	Medium risk
5	233		Low risk
6	3.4	World class	Almost zero risk

Figure 9-9 Why assessing behavioral risk is a critical business metric

To focus on the level of "system" risk, which should be of concern to both management and those responsible for oversight and governance, an equivalent level of risk can be attributed to the maturity ratings based on the equivalent (approximate) risks related to creditworthiness. Using a tool such as OMINDEX® would enable organizations to establish a metric that linked culture to behavior and then to organizational risk (Figure 9.10). Considering how many decisions are made daily by people, operating with no stated "code of expectations" is a high risk - especially in a world of flattening organizations, delegation, sub-contracting, client focus and agility of decision making.

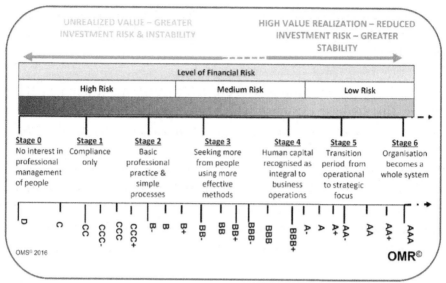

Figure 9-10 Linking organizational and behavioral risk to OMINDEX® ratings

While a colour chart would make the risk clearer, the left-hand side of **High Risk** is depicted as red, tapering to amber across **Medium Risk** and then to green at the **Low Risk** area. While this may not be a perfect solution, it does start to demonstrate the criticality and opportunity related to human capital.

This simple, single rating applied to human capital provides an alternative to the single, holistic performance measure of profit expressed in financial terms. Research and experience from the Maturity Institute, which developed the conceptual models and background research, and the Organizational Maturity Services, LLP (OMS), which has been heavily involved not only in deploying the OMINDEX® ratings but also working with organizations to identify improvements in areas such as output, growth, revenue, and quality, has revealed a significant opportunity to enhance and grow margins.

What about the practical reality of using this indicator? Have any results been created that indicate the value in addressing risk at the system level from organizations that might appear healthy using traditional approaches?

The first example is Handelsbanken, which was mentioned in the last chapter. This Swedish business, which refers to itself as a Personal Banking Company, was one of the earliest organizations assessed using the OMINDEX®. In 2015, the company was assessed at an "A" rating and in 2017 it scored "AA", at which time it had an overall score of 82.6%. The Maturity Institute refers to the company as one of its "exemplars," reflecting well on aspects of a human-centric culture. In 2017, Handelsbanken was included in a global "Banking and Governance" report that looked at 20 global banks, which were assessed asking the following:

> *Have any of the banks performed better since the global financial crisis in 2008? Has there been any discernible, positive shift in governance and the health of their cultures? Do their CEOs exhibit greater integrity? Do the banks pose less risk? If so, has this translated into higher value for investors, customers, employees and wider stakeholders?*

Handelsbanken scored at the top of the list, while 12 other banks scored below the median of 47% (half the rating of the leader). A high score using the OMINDEX® rating would appear to align with an organization that has a core set of values that drive its behavior and that this approach results in superior performance. Would such an indicator applied to the other banks indicate any underlying risk related to behavior?

The second example is from a 2016 assessment carried out on AT&T (using credit rating information from 2015):

> *AT&T's OMR rating of B+ indicates a relatively low level of maturity with incipient signs of organizational instability and unnecessary levels of risk. Minimal recognition of the potential value opportunity*

available from its own 280,000 employees, or those employed within its supply chain, is evidenced, or exhibited. No clear Human Capital strategy is outlined, and its management policies and practices reveal no prior, underlying hypothesis to justify their use in business value terms.

At the time of this assessment, AT&T was in the early stages of acquiring DirectTV as a way of diversifying into media and alternative delivery. At the time, the company credit rating was about BBB but the OMINDEX® assessment was lower at about B+. This difference in ratings can be considered a "risk gap" – while traditional metrics indicate limited risk, the OMINDEX® suggest a much higher risk as well as an opportunity (as discussed in the *Costs of Poor Culture* book, low rankings would indicate higher probability of financial surprises, hidden costs, and lost opportunities, all of which depress performance in financial capital – i.e., profit). Figure 9.11 shows a comparison between traditional credit (financial ratings) and the OMINDEX® system.

Since this report was developed, the AT&T performance has not significantly improved and investors have not seen the expected benefits from the DirectTV merger; in fact, having lost considerable financial capital, the company now plans to sell its media activities. Had investors used the "whole system" OMINDEX® metric together with the risks identified relative to integration, many would have been pre-warned about the impending loss of financial capital caused by inattention to human capital and the creation of a culture within which performance can be optimized. It is also worth noting that, from a social / benefit to society perspective, AT&T appears to have lost 50,000 jobs in the last five years, with its current headcount at 230,000.

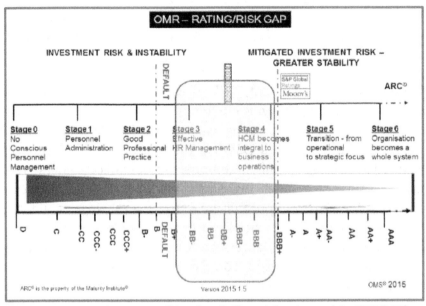

*Figure 9-11 Comparison between traditional credit (financial) ratings and the OMINDEX®
(system) demonstrates a risk gap*

All the materials discussed in this chapter are available in much greater
detail by either accessing the websites of the organizations mentioned
above or by reading the book, *The Mature Corporation*[39]. The search for
enhanced metrics, including a much greater focus on human capital will be
an important part of developing a new approach to corporate governance
and accountability.

---

[39] Kearns, Paul, and Woollard, Stuart, *The Mature Corporation: A Model of Responsible
Capitalism*, 2019, Cambridge Scholars Publishing.

Total system - summary
• A poor culture can have hidden risks and problems which are invisible to key stakeholders.
• A major type of risk results in financial surprises caused by unexpected behaviors.
• Organizational culture is a risk management approach to reduce the potential of financial surprises.
• Traditional audits and financial reporting fail to warn against underlying operational problems.
• A human capital metric developed around people-centricity, would provide an added level of risk awareness to stakeholders.
• The OMINDEX® rating system is one example of a human-centric whole system metric that provides a composite measure of performance.
• Use of such metrics might well provide a better evaluation of performance than current HC ROI.
Total system - checklist
• Does the organization primarily rely on profit as its measure of whole system performance?
• Have there been occasions when an unexpected employee decision has had unplanned negative results?
• Has the organization explored other metrics for whole system "health and quality" that reflect a people-centric reality?

10 Conclusion

This book has covered a great deal of ground. Human capital metrics – especially as they relate to the integration of human capital into an integrated reporting framework – are in their infancy. There are many human performance metrics available but, to date, they are not well-integrated, either into high-level business goals or to the inter-relationship with other capitals.

Developing and implementing human capital metrics should be seen as an activity that parallels the evolution of human resources management from a functional focus to a strategically driven and enterprise-wide commitment to human capital. Some may feel uncomfortable in this transition, yet it offers one of the major opportunities to create significant competitive advantage. People really are an organization's greatest asset but creating an environment that engages people rather than relying on "command and control" is an extremely challenging task.

Managers at all levels might feel like they are giving up their power and risking a loss of control. Some have used the phrase that "empowering employees" is like turning the prison over to the prisoners. Many managers compensation packages are heavily tied to business outcomes, yet many do not consider the impact on human capital in achieving these outcomes. Managers feel very nervous and worry that employee engagement is like letting go of control. So, the journey towards a more human-centric / human capital-oriented organization will be difficult.

There is also the misapprehension, currently being seen, that developing metrics is a standalone activity not tied into the strategic activities of the business. Some organizations feel that HR should "stay within its boundaries" and not try and get involved in the operational aspects of people deployment and leadership. This is akin to two other historic evolutions of functional specializations that faced similar challenges:

- Accounting used to be relegated to the "back office" to "keep the records," until the evolution of management accounting. Once it was realized that accountants could add value to the business by creating a better understanding of financial decisions, the profession became central to business decision making.
- Quality management used to focus on compliance to specifications and ensuring inspections were carried out to avoid defective products being shipped to clients. Once it was realized that quality had to be "built into" products and services through every activity that took place in the organization, quality became a strategic issue. It was now everyone's job – not a functional responsibility.

This is the place of human resources today; it is no longer about compliance and administering the processes necessary to provide people to the organization. People have become the single largest value-creating resource in many organizations. Optimizing human capital is the job of everyone, starting at the highest level.

Consultants say that to be effective "you have to start where the client is." In other words, every organization is at a point of reality that will determine what steps are required to move forward and evolve. The journey has a few key goals that this book has tried to develop:

1. Start with where you are – use existing metrics, including searching around for things that are already being tracked.
2. Start to ask what the HR metrics are showing and whether it creates value. Most metrics are of little value if they are not capable of

being compared, i.e., this is where we are versus where we planned to be, whether it be turnover, cycle time for recruitment or number of grievances filed.

3. Research the direction of external human capital reporting *in addition* to mandatory reporting requirements (one seeks statutory compliance but the other seeks insight into the value creation ability of people).

4. Start to build a metrics framework that aligns with the business model of inputs, activities, outputs and outcomes.

5. Approach the development of human capital metrics using a strategic life-cycle approach, founded upon the Plan, Do, Check and Act approach.

6. Ensure that business planning clearly identifies the expected outcomes of an effective human-centric approach and use these expected outcomes as the basis for creating metrics at the input, activity, and output stages; i.e., they should be a set of outcomes that clearly demonstrate right people, right place, right time, right performance, and optimum effectiveness.

7. Ensure that human capital planning is driven not only by the skills and capabilities required for the outputs and outcomes required, but also (equally) by the creation of a workplace where these people can work at optimum performance.

Finally, although culture may be seen as a human resources issue, it is not; while the CHRO may lead the charge for developing a human-centric organization, it cannot happen without the governance of the organization – the "G" in ESG – making people central to value creation and risk management, typically the Board, and the CEO ensuring that leadership messages are defined by expectations, reinforced by leaders at all levels, firmly embedded in every aspect of operational activity, recognized and rewarded. And above all, governance should be consistent so that a foundation of integrity and trust can be established.

This is the future and opportunity for putting people at the centre of value creation, sustainability, and organizational resilience. This is where culture lives and it is the strategic change that must be made to ensure the development and use of human capital metrics becomes more than a numbers exercise.

As a final note – the goal to aim for will be few metrics – maybe just turnover and engagement (plus statutory requirements). As Drucker said, *"Culture eats strategy for breakfast."* Once you get the right culture in place and every single person, partner, and stakeholder aligned with and supporting *both* purpose and values, then an organization will have a sustainable competitive advantage. On top of this, they will need far fewer metrics because people will effectively become self-managing and self-optimizing.

Acknowledgements

This book would not be complete without thanks and acknowledgements to many of the people who have provided thoughts, ideas, and inspiration over the years. My awakening about the importance of people in organizations may have developed in my very early years, when I worked in our family grocery business, where the staff were friends and part of an extended family – all apparently committed to making the business work.

I lost this linkage after my family lost the business as a result of medical issues, leading to financial collapse. After this, my early career in accounting also failed to re-kindle it, but when I joined a technology company in the 1970s, I started to realize the impact of human creativity and knowledge on innovation and growth, and how running a business "by the numbers" can put this human capital at risk. These were heady days, as we designed and built some of the first semiconductors – chips – when the technology was advancing at an unprecedented rate.

From this point on, I tried to balance financial and human management, but this all came crashing down when, the mainframe computer and computer services company, of which I was CFO, was faced with major downsizing. Walt LeGrow, VP of Human Resources at the time, advised me well over those years, but I'm sorry to say Walt, that much of this advice fell on stony ground.

My next really important lesson was as President of a distribution company, where I came to realize the importance of people and the relationships that they build that make business happen. I also realized that not having anyone in charge of the "people" part of the business is a major issue, and that HR policies, processes, and management *are* important. You only realize the value of something when you don't have it. To all the employees of Canadian Bearings or, as it is now, CB, thanks for the guidance and experience. This did, however, give me the opportunity to build and develop a foundation of organizational values as well as what we then called an Integrated Human Resource Management System (IHRMS). The values became the foundation of how we approached the running of the business, and the IHRMS became the framework for working toward cohesiveness and consistency of expectations, and fairness.

After setting up my own business, I started to work with Dr. Peter Smyth; I did process management, while he did the "soft stuff." Peter taught me that the soft stuff is in fact the hard stuff. He also made me realize that frustrating though the process maybe, employee engagement is critical to effective process management and human commitment to an organization's goals.

During these years, I worked with many people linked with, and involved in, people leadership and management. There are way too many to remember them all, but some I would like to single out: Dr. Stewart Desson of Lumina Learning (UK), together with Janice Parviainen of Lumina Canada, the US, Australia, and New Zealand; Paul Kearns and Stuart Woollard from The Maturity Institute in the UK; Mary Adams from Smarter Companies; Dr. Ken Standfield, now of Strategic Time Management (Australia); the late Dwaine Eamer from Electrical Inspection / Ontario Hydro; Suzanne Court; Rod Barr; Guy Gordon (from our work at the Institute of Citizen Centred Service), together with Faye Schmidt and Karen Prokopec.

Finally, in the last few years, the following have proved invaluable: Neil McCormick, ISO TC 260 Working group 2, and the rest of the members of that team; Amy Armitage, Founder and Co-Chair Human Capital Investment and Reporting Council (HC-IRC), and members of that group; Lee Webster (USA), Hilger Pothmann (Germany), Jeff Higgins (USA), Brad Boyson (UAE), Karl Craven and Wilson Wong (UK); and Solange Charas, Heather Whiteman, Doug Hoppe, and Zahid Mubarik, all of Human Capital Impact (HCM-I).

Long may the journey continue. One of the greatest wastes in life is the waste of human talent and opportunity. It is the duty of every one of us to bring out the best in others and to work and act in a way that supports the health and well-being of everyone.

Bibliography

Adams, Mary, and Oleksak, Michael, *Intangible Capital*, 2010, Praeger.

Becker, Brian. E., Huselid, Mark. A., and Ulrich, F. Dave. *The HR Scorecard*, 2001, Harvard Business Press.

Brooking, Annie, *Intellectual Capital*, 1996, International Thomson Business Press.

Brooking, Annie, *Corporate memory*, 1999, International Thomson Business Press.

Bowman. C. W., *Intangibles*, 2005, Grafiks Books.

Buckingham, Marcus, and Coffman, Curt, *First, Break All The Rules: What the World's Greatest Managers Do Differently*, 1999, Gallup / Simon & Schuster.

Davenport, Thomas. H., and Prusak, Laurence, *Working Knowledge*, 1998, Harvard Business School Press.

Eden, Jeremy, and Long, Terri, *Low-Hanging Fruit: 77 Eye-Opening Ways to Improve Productivity and Profits*, 2014, Wiley.

Edvinsson, Leif, and Malone, Michael S., *Intellectual Capital*, 1997, Harper Business.

Ehin, Charles, *Unleashing Intellectual Capital*, 2000, Butterworth-Heinmann.

Fitz-enz, Jac, *The ROI of Human Capital*, 2000, AMACOM.

Galloway, Scott, *The Four – the hidden DNA of Amazon, Apple, Facebook and Google*, 2017, Portfolio – Penguin.

Gertz, Dwight L., and Baptista, João P.A., *Grow to be Great*, 1995, Free Press.

Gleeson-White, Jane, *Six Capitals*, 2014, Allen & Unwin (Australia).

Goldratt, Eli, *Theory of Constraints*, 1999, North River Press.

Goldratt, Eli, *The Goal*, 1982 (Revised 2012), North River Press.

Hand, John, and Lev, Baruch, *Intangible Assets: Values, Measures and Risk*, 2003, Oxford University Press.

Haskel, Jonathan, and Westlake, Stan, *Capitalism Without Capital*, 2018, Princeton University Press.

IIRC (International Integrated Reporting Council; now the Value Foundation), *Creating Value: The value of human capital reporting*, 2016, As of Oct 2021, at the Creating Value series of publications https://www.integratedreporting.org/resource/creating-value-board/

IIRC (International Integrated Reporting Council; now the Value Foundation), *The <IR> Framework* (as of October 2021 at https://www.integratedreporting.org/resource/international-ir-framework/

Kaplan, Robert. S., and Norton, David. P., *Alignment*, 2006, Harvard Business School Publishing.

Kaplan, Robert. S., and Norton, David. P., *The Balanced Scorecard*, 1996, Harvard Business Press.

Kearns, Paul, and Woollard, Stuart, *The Mature Corporation: A Model for Responsible Capitalism*, 2019, Cambridge Scholars Press.

Low, Jonathan, and Kalafut, Pam Cohen, *Invisible advantage*, 2002, Berkeley Books.

Schmidt, Eric, and Rosenberg, Jonathan, *Google: How Google Works*, 2014, Hachette Book Group.

Shepherd, Nick. A., and Smyth, Peter. J., *Reflective Leaders and High-Performance Organizations,*" 2012, iUniverse.

Shepherd, Nick, *Corporate Culture – Combining values and purpose*, 2021, Eduvision Inc. / Jannas Publications, KDP / Amazon.

Shepherd, Nick, *How Accountants Lost their Balance*, 2021, Eduvision Inc. Jannas Publications, KDP / Amazon.

Shepherd, Nick, *The Cost of Poor Culture*, 2021, Eduvision Inc. / Jannas Publications, KDP / Amazon.

Shepherd, Nick A., *Governance, Accountability and Sustainable Development*, 2005, Thomson Canada.

Shepherd, N., and Adams, Mary, *Unrecognized Intangible Assets: Identification, Management and Reporting*, 2010, IMA Statements in Management Accounting.

Standfield, Ken, *Intangible Management*, 2002, Academic Press.

Stewart, Thomas. A., *Intellectual Capital*, 1997, Currency Doubleday.

Sullivan, Patrick. H., *Value-driven intellectual capital*, 2000, Wiley.

Sveiby, Karl Erik, *The New Organizational Wealth*, 1997, Berrett-Koehler.

Waterman, Robert H., Jr., and Peters, Tom, In Search of Excellence: Lessons from America's Best-Run Companies, 2015, Collins Business Essentials

Weiss, David. S., *High Performance HR*, 2000, Wiley.

NICK A. SHEPHERD
FCPA, FCGA, FCCA, FCMC,

Nick has over 50 years of varied work experience including senior general management and finance roles. From 1989 to 2017 he ran his own management consulting and professional development company. Currently, he is officially retired but still spends time on research and writing, focusing his efforts in the areas of organizational sustainability, human capital, and integrated reporting. Nick has experience working in, and with private family business, public corporations, governments, and NPOs. Nick is currently a Director and Council member of the UK-based Maturity Institute.

As a management consultant and facilitator, Nick designed and presented many professional development workshops internationally, and across Canada. Nick was also part-time faculty member at Grenoble Graduate School of Business (GGSB), where he taught modules on Mergers and Acquisitions, and Management Consulting; Nick also lectured at McMaster / DeGroote on ethics. Nick led the Professional Standards Committee of the International Council of Management Consultants in developing the competency model that now forms the basis of CMC certification in over 50 global CMC Institutes. In 2007, Nick received the President's Award for Education from the Certified General Accountants of British Columbia. Nick's consulting work included both public and private sector clients in many countries including Canada, the USA, the UK, the Caribbean, South Africa, Kazakhstan, Kyrgyzstan, Uzbekistan, and Jordan.

Nick joined CPA Ontario as a Fellow in 2014 following the merger of accounting bodies. Prior to that Nick was a CGA for over 35 years, obtaining his Fellowship in 2009. Nick is a Fellow of the Chartered Association of Certified Accountants (FCCA UK), and a Fellow of the Institute of Certified Management Consultants of Ontario (FCMC – Honour Roll), and Past President of the Institute. Nick is Past Chair of the National Certification Committee for all Institutes of Management Consulting across Canada, and Past Chair of the Professional Standards Committee of the International Council of Management Consulting Institutes (ICMCI). He served as one of four trustees for Canada at the International level (ICMCI). Nick has also been a member of Mensa for many years.

Nick has written a number of books; he is co-author of *Reflective Leaders and High Performing Organizations*, written in 2012 with Dr. Peter Smyth. Nick also wrote *Governance, Accountability and Sustainable Development* in 2005, dealing with Governance issues for the 21st century, and the *Controllers Handbook* (now in its 2nd edition). These books add to a number of other books and articles that Nick has authored, including *Values and Ethics: From Inception to Practice, The Evolution of Accountability – Sustainability Reporting for Accountants, Unrecognized Intangible Assets: Identification, Management and Reporting*, and *The Human Aspects of Cost Control*. Nick also developed several Ethics courses for accountants and consultants, nationally and internationally.

Contact Nick at nick@eduvision.ca